BUOYANT CLARITY

Pamphlet Architecture 36

Princeton Architectural Press, New York

MEYER / HEMMENDINGER / MEYER
christopher   daniel   shawna

Published by
Princeton Architectural Press
A McEvoy Group company
202 Warren Street, Hudson, NY 12534
Visit our website at www.papress.com

Princeton Architectural Press is a leading publisher
in architecture, design, photography, landscape, and
visual culture. We create fine books and stationery of
unsurpassed quality and production values. With more
than one thousand titles published, we find design
everywhere and in the most unlikely places.

This project is supported in part by an award from
the National Endowment for the Arts.

Editors: Simone Kaplan-Senchak and Nolan Boomer
Designers: Daniel Hemmendinger, Christopher Meyer,
and Shawna Meyer

Special thanks to: Ryan Alcazar, Janet Behning,
Abby Bussel, Benjamin English, Jan Cigliano Hartman,
Susan Hershberg, Kristen Hewitt, Lia Hunt,
Valerie Kamen, Jennifer Lippert, Sara McKay,
Eliana Miller, Nina Pick, Wes Seeley, Rob Shaeffer,
Sara Stemen, Marisa Tesoro, Paul Wagner, and
Joseph Weston of Princeton Architectural Press
—Kevin C. Lippert, publisher

Library of Congress Cataloging-in-Publication Data

Names: Meyer, Christopher, author. | Meyer, Shawna,
author. | Hemmendinger, Daniel, author.
Title: Pamphlet Architecture 36 : Buoyant Clarity /
Christopher Meyer, Daniel Hemmendinger, and
Shawna Meyer.
Description: First edition. | New York : Princeton
Architectural Press, 2018.
Identifiers: LCCN 2017040828 | ISBN 9781616896430
(paperback)
Subjects: LCSH: City planning—Climatic factors. |
Floating cities. | BISAC: ARCHITECTURE / General.
Classification: LCC NA9053.E58 M49 2018 | DDC
720—dc23
LC record available at https://lccn.loc.gov/2017040828

Amphibious Space

an essay by the authors

04

I. Waiting to Leave

Morphing Edges

Deconstructing Urbanism

Shipbreakers

Filtration Buoyage

18

In Parallel

*a conversation with Vincent James,
FAIA, and Jennifer Yoos, FAIA*

12

amphibious space

The word *amphibian* comes from the Greek term *amphibios* and means "living a double life." Reconciling the definition, meaning, and connotations of *amphibian* allows for a dynamic reading of a potential amphibious space. On the one hand, we can understand something amphibious as being related to and suitable for both land and water. On the other, a "double life" implies a fragile relationship between land and sea: two contexts wholly separated, perhaps a secret kept, waiting to all fall apart. An amphibian, therefore, is a transitional figure inhabiting a space not just where land and water meet, but where they overlap and claim each other.

Planet Earth, projection from the South Pole.

Between land and sea lies a space in flux: a coastal zone. The coast is unequivocally land, but it is land built up, slurried, and shaped by water, a strange intermediary muddling the binary. Across the planet, entire nations can increasingly be understood less as masses of land and more as expanses of coastal, or littoral, space—areas tenuously inhabited and increasingly at risk due to sea-level rise. An architecture for both land and sea will be necessary in these contexts as seas rise from ice melt and the thermal expansion of water, placing over 600 million people at risk globally.[1] While retreating to higher ground nearby may be a possibility for many, it may not be possible for those in some large cities sitting in low-lying zones on islands where higher elevations to relocate do not exist.

Tarawa, the capital of Kiribati, is home to over 50,000 people, and its highest point reaches a mere three meters above sea level. Malé, the capital of the Maldives, has a population of over 150,000 people and a high point of 2.4 meters. In addition, many islands with smaller populations lie in similarly threatened contexts. Along the Intracoastal Waterway, the sinew that ties the Louisiana Gulf Coast to land, populations along low-lying inlets, rivers, and canals negotiate the risks of fluctuating environmental conditions, while sections of New Orleans, a city with approximately 390,000 residents, lie as much as five meters below sea level.[2] Humanity's desire to isolate environmental pressures in these sites has historically manifested itself in constructed boundaries—levees, seawalls, and the like—yet a more thorough interrogation of water, and the forms and techniques we use to inhabit it, can inform how people live in these low-lying settlements in meaningful and long-lasting ways.

The rapid pace of environmental change is shifting the balance of territory from a land-dominant condition to a water-dominant one, raising complicated questions about the idea of place. Yet while it is fair to wonder what will happen to specific settlements, it is more important to ask: What will happen to all of these people? Will they decide to leave or to stay? If they leave, where will they go? If they stay, how will they adapt?

AQUA FIRMA

Modern history demonstrates humanity's indifference toward and, at times, contempt for the sea. By isolating ourselves to land, rather than embracing a transitional and multivalent form of living, humans have disregarded and relinquished responsibility for the care and stewardship of the hydrosphere. Illegal dumping, pollution, and man-made disasters amass slowly but relentlessly in the ocean's five gyres.[3] Even natural disasters in the form of hurricanes and tsunamis, while known for the damage they do on land, also drag debris and refuse out to sea, perhaps to be discovered years later on foreign shores. More likely, though, the waste will silently gather in the oceans, disintegrate over time, contaminate ecosystems, and enter food chains, slowly and persistently disrupting marine biomes and natural processes. Humanity's actions demonstrate a perspective preoccupied with the stabilization, construction, and reconstruction of solid ground—a hydrophobic lifestyle. They also foreground our penchant for short-term resolution at the expense of long-term advancement, a present divorced from its consequences.

The term *terra firma* originated in the 1600s to describe the territories on the mainland of Italy controlled by the state of Venice.[4] This distinction—between "firm land" and a Venetian other—highlights a specific way of thinking about the spatial character of Venice itself. Situated in a lagoon, traversing 118 islands, and at once divided and linked by a network of canals, Venice embodies an amphibious worldview in which the fluctuations of water levels are invited into the space of the city and accommodated through the techniques and technologies of its time. Giving primacy to water and its natural variation is increasingly relevant today and holds new potential for innovation within our time. We should design for *aqua firma*.

Generally, planning approaches to amphibious spaces depend on a culture's philosophical attitude: is this space a softer form of a terrestrial zone or an extension of a hydrological system? In terrestrially focused cultures, lowlands are fortified by constructing levees, raised platforms, pump stations, and other infrastructure, or by claiming new land—confusingly called land "reclamation." Architectures in this paradigm benefit from these various fortifications, but they must also take additional measures to alleviate risk. Operational moves, like lifting and mounding, or situational appliqué, like flotation devices, leave the original architecture largely intact and suggest little in the way of innovation or responsibility. Implicitly, they endanger their inhabitants through increased structural eccentricity and denial of latent risks like flooding or erosion.

By contrast, recognizing coastal space as relating to a water-based ecology—aqua firma—produces distinct infrastructures and architectures. Locks, canals, and other devices that give primacy to seaborne transport are

5

matched with floating structures, architectural accommodation of water's ebbs and flows, and other aquatic strategies. This attitude is seen in many coastal vernacular architectures, but contemporary "designed" examples that embrace this attitude generally treat the water's edge as a permanent site for an attached terrestrial inhabitation. Aldo Rossi's Teatro del Mondo (1979) and Google's floating barges, reportedly to serve as Google Glass stores, were mobile, or at least intended to be so, but can be viewed as wholly grounded structures built on seafaring platforms. Both solutions demonstrate an awareness of their contexts, but a fundamental discomfort with subsisting there. Contemporary examples of architecture that are designed to be seafaring and renounce barging have often proven perilous, overambitious, or naive about the associated monetary and material costs.[5] Louis Kahn's floating concert hall, Point Counterpoint II (completed in 1976, after his death), is an outlier. Its different orientations for performance and movement suggest a design sensibility rooted in a considered relationship between land and water.

The occupation of amphibious space has historically been temporary, and often as a consequence of economic, political, or agricultural forces. More recently, oceans have been spaces to cast away the unwanted, serving as both dumping ground and landless exile. In 1987, the *Mobro 4000* barge left Islip, New York, with three thousand tons of unwanted waste and spent the next six weeks traveling six thousand miles to multiple ports, national and international, unable to offload onto land.[6] In 1991, thousands of Albanian refugees fled aboard the vessel *Vlora* to the Italian coast, where they were unable to negotiate acceptance into the city of Bari and were left bound to

their vessel, stranded at sea.[7] Early in 2009, Burmese and Bangladeshi asylum seekers were pulled out into the Andaman Sea by Thai soldiers and left to drift aimlessly, and in 2015, vessels holding thousands of Rohingya migrants were held in the Andaman Sea while political authorities from the countries of Indonesia, Thailand, and Malaysia refused to accept the "boat people."[8] By shifting the narrative to one of intention, it is possible to imagine modes of inhabitation that foster an enduring relationship with water, encouraging nimbleness and responsibility. Likewise, rather than prescribe a single result for a particular choice, or naively advocate for a solution within oppressive and often racist geopolitical realities, architecture should be responsible for a multiplicity of possible outcomes: staying or leaving, planned or haphazard.

Human occupation of amphibious space relies on two complementary concepts: buoyancy and anchorage. Buoyancy, by definition, relies on density. Buoyant objects possess a net force in a fluid that allows for the defiance of gravitational pull. Anchorage—while a compressive force on land—is tensile in water, due to the upward force of a buoyant object or the pull of lateral forces on the anchored object. To that end, anchorage cannot exist without buoyancy in amphibious space. Likewise, buoyant objects possess the capacity for anchorage in almost any case, whether it be moorings or anchors for ships or tethering for buoys, or other forms of buoyant platforms.

BUOYANCY

In a technical sense, the term *buoyancy* simply describes the tendency to float in or rise to the surface of a fluid. But it is also charged with connotations of agility, movement, flexibility,

and adaptation. Buoyancy is an expression of optimism and hope. To be buoyant is to be confident, enthusiastic, and persistent in design thinking. Spatial rules define the fluid environment through strata, with buoyancy as the uppermost surface and anchorage as the bottom, together framing an intermediate zone of suspension. A survey of humankind's innovations related to buoyage, buoyant objects, and our relationship to aquatic life demonstrates the limited palette of techniques we possess and exposes the shortcomings of a predominantly terrestrial agenda. While the conversation is often anthropocentric, with short and definitive timelines aimed at achieving specific ends—extraction and transportation of resources, temporary leisure, data collection, war, or commerce—there are a number of useful exceptions.

Just as infrastructures, architectures, and utilities establish orders and organizations in quotidian life on land, the sea is virtually and materially described through similar impositions. Oil rigs are the sea's extraction sites, shipping routes its highways, vessels its 18-wheelers, and buoys its road signs and weather vanes. The buoy's potential to accumulate uses and meaning within an increasingly seafaring paradigm circumscribes a new ground upon which amphibious spaces emerge and proliferate. Its ability to function in tandem with other buoys and vessels—and tap into weather and bathymetric data—can make it a live navigational tool for inhabitants of amphibious space. The buoy can also clean the waters it drifts in, operating as a steward of its environment, and can communicate not only whom it belongs to but also the histories of the places it has been. Networked into a field condition with similar actors, the buoy plays an orientational and phenomenological role.

[2] Gordon McGranahan, Deborah Balk, and Bridget Anderson, "The Rising Tide: Assessing the Risks of Climate Change and Human Settlements in Low Elevation Coastal Zones," *Environment and Urbanization* 19, no. 1 (2007): 24.

[3] Joel K. Bourne Jr., "New Orleans: A Perilous Future." *National Geographic*, August 2007, http://ngm.nationalgeographic.com/2007/08/new-orleans/new-orleans-text.

[4] Laura Parker, "Ocean Trash: 5.25 Trillion Pieces and Counting, but Big Questions Remain," *National Geographic*, January 11, 2015, http://news.nationalgeographic.com/news/2015/01/150109-oceans-plastic-sea-trash-science-marine-debris.

[5] Douglas Harper, Online Etymology Dictionary, s.v. "terra firma," accessed August 28, 2017, http://www.etymonline.com/index.php?term=terra+firma.

[6] NLÉ's Makoko Floating School collapsed in a thunderstorm in 2016. Recent proposals from the Seasteading Institute aimed at "middle-income buyers" carry a construction cost of $978 per square foot, more than six times the rate to build a conventional home.

[7] Philip S. Gutis, "L.I.'s Garbage Now an Issue for Diplomats," *New York Times*, April 25, 1987.

[8] David Binder, "Thousands of Albanians Flee Aboard Ships to Italy," *New York Times*, March 6, 1991.

[9] Subir Bhaumik, "Thais 'Leave Boat People to Die,'" *BBC News*, January 15, 2009, http://news.bbc.co.uk/1/hi/world/south_asia/7830710.stm. Euan McKirdy and Saima Mohsin, "Unwanted: The Plight of Myanmar's Rohingya Boat People," *CNN*, May 19, 2015, http://www.cnn.com/2015/05/19/asia/rohingya-refugee-ships-explainer.

Top, *Stilts allow fishermen in Sri Lanka to occupy the sea while minimizing the lateral effect of waves;* bottom, *Designed explorations of aquatic occupation have been more recreationally oriented, but offer visceral relationships with water.*

The buoy's architectural value should also be noted. The R/P *FLIP*, a 108-meter-long research vessel launched in 1962, is designed to pitch forward in the water and sit perpendicular to the surface, allowing it to study the density and temperature of water, measure wave height, and collect meteorological data seventeen meters above and ninety-one meters below the surface.[9] This action of flipping allows the vessel to function as a spar buoy, reducing its susceptibility to wave action. Considered as architecture, the R/P *FLIP* is inhabitable in two orientations, resulting in unique details, spaces, and technical solutions. Stairs in one orientation are banisters in another, delimiting a floor that becomes a wall. Showerheads curve, the toilet seat rotates, and the resulting space is thickened both perceptually and conceptually.[10] The novelty of the R/P *FLIP*'s rotation in water suggests a trajectory for a fluid and nimble mode of design thinking in amphibious space.

Ocean liners, warships, and large cargo vessels are fabricated and repaired in dry docks: amphibious spaces where seafaring vessels can be constructed and repaired on dry ground— suitable to human physiology and ergonomics. Dry docks can be built into intermediary zones as hydrophilic land depressions. Other dry docks are free floating, transforming them conceptually into seaborne extensions of land. As humankind's ocean vessels become larger and larger, we can increasingly understand them as grounds themselves. The largest ship ever built, an oil tanker called *Seawise Giant*, at 458 meters long and 69 meters wide, is hardly an outlier.[11] Existing specifications for Valemax and New Panamax vessel typologies, today's standard cargo and ore carrier vessels, are comparable to those of a Manhattan block, while Super Post-Panamax gantries, already in

service, hint at a future even longer and wider. Shell's *Prelude*, a floating liquefied natural gas platform, is categorically known as a VLFS (a very large floating structure), which measures 488 meters long by 74 meters wide.[12]

Also in the VLFS category, and the longest floating structure ever built, the Megafloat project produced a thousand-meter-long runway in Tokyo Bay to prototype floating structures for the ongoing construction of Kansai International Airport.[13] The Megafloat's scale blurs the boundary between buoyant object and land, offering an alternative to "land reclamation" and suggesting the possibility of floating human settlements with concentrated densities of people, similar to cities on land.

ANCHORAGE

An amphibious architecture can also be anchored or moored, reaching down through the water in search of terra firma. Anchorage involves securing oneself to something fixed to facilitate stasis above for a variety of timescales. A tethered inhabitation can be anchored until the connection to land is no longer tenable, and then detach and remain seaborne until new land is allocated or perhaps political objections subside. Aquatic territory can provide economic support for communities adrift, through the repurposing of obsolete infrastructural networks and retired technologies, allowing them to subsist on water.

Piers and jetties are one type of anchorage that allows people to access deeper water sites near land for sustenance, recreation, and the boarding of seafaring vessels. They can range in degree of permanence, from infilled extensions of land like Lower Manhattan and Back Bay, Boston, to temporary infrastructures

[9] "R/P *FLIP*: Technical Details," Scripps Institution of Oceanography, accessed May 18, 2017, https://scripps.ucsd.edu/ships/flip /technical.

[10] Randy Christian, "R/V *Sally Ride*: Report from the *FLIP*," Scripps Institution of Oceanography, March 20, 2017, https://scripps.ucsd .edu/expeditions/sallyride/2017/03/20/report-from-the-flip.

[11] "*Seawise Giant*—the Biggest Ship Ever Built," Vessel Tracking, accessed May 28, 2017, http://www.vesseltracking.net/article /seawise-giant.

[12] David Shukman, "The Largest Vessel the World Has Ever Seen," *BBC News*, December 16, 2014, http://www.bbc.com/news/science -environment-30394137.

[13] David Russell Schilling, "The World's Largest Floating Airport, Tokyo Bay's Megafloat," *Industry Tap*, May 17, 2013, http://www .industrytap.com/worlds-largest-floating-airport-in-tokyo-bay/3684.

The dry dock, in all of its various forms, derives from a conventional understanding of mooring defined by a terrestrial floor. The R/P FLIP, in contrast, deploys an awareness of more complex rules of physics, shifting to a vertical orientation to float in place.

such as Christo's *The Floating Piers* installation (2016) or the barges built for the Festa del Redentore in Venice. Connectors, another type of anchorage, offer a strong interrelation between land and sea and also demonstrate the potential for architecture to establish and territorialize an amphibious space. In many contexts around the globe, floating houses exist within a space of flux, delineating architectural grounds for a double life. Critical to a connector's success is a flexible relationship between the aquatic environment, the anchoring mechanism, and the anchored object. Anchored or tethered objects interface with the water, in constant fluctuation; water must be allowed to move fluidly around the tethered object. Conversely, the anchored object must not expect a static relationship with the aquatic environment, requiring certain planning and predicting of the allowable range of movement.

The jack-up rig is a notable example. Also known as a self-elevating platform, the jack-up rig consists of an inhabited platform (or hull), a system of flotation devices, and a set of supports capable of anchorage and suspension. The jack-up rig functions as both an anchored and a buoyant object. When anchored, the long support legs are lowered down through the water to stand on solid ground. The platform is then free to move itself hydraulically up and down the support legs, providing a dynamic response to a variety of possible conditions. When buoyant, the platform floats, allowing it to move where it is needed or desired. While jack-up barges are industrial tools used for the extraction of resources or for accessing objects at sea, the potential to translate this technique to inhabitation in increasingly amphibious zones offers flexibility and a measure of safety.

BLUER PASTURES

While only inhabiting 32 percent of the earth's surface, humanity has massively affected the global climate balance, calling into question whether we are ready for a life in which we are free to inhabit all 100 percent. The decision for humankind to leave its home for bluer pastures is laden with difficult questions and harsh realities. Can place exist without ground? Can a nation exist without territory? Can the oceans be regarded as a new beginning when they are filled with the oil slicks and floating refuse of humanity's excesses? Tectonic knowledge and basic assumptions on land will not be directly transferrable to an existence on aqua firma. Nor will amphibious living directly resemble terrestrial life. Questioning today's fundamental societal practices, like power generation, manufacturing, waste creation and management, agricultural cultivation and distribution, and livestock production will be part and parcel of a commitment to an amphibious existence.

An apt case study in planning for coastal populations can be found in Saint Mary Parish and Terrebonne Parish, Louisiana, specifically in the communities of Isle de Jean Charles, Cocodrie, and Morgan City. The State of Louisiana has found itself on the front lines in addressing the relocation of the committed residents of Isle de Jean Charles, who remain on land that the sea has come to claim. A statement by Chief Albert Naquin of the Biloxi-Chitimacha-Choctaw Band, native to the land, summarizes the impact: "We're going to lose all our heritage, all our culture. . . . It's all going to be history."[14]

The Isle de Jean Charles Resettlement Project is the first American program to attempt the relocation of an entire community.[15] Those in charge of developing the program, which aims to "ensure a historically contextual and culturally appropriate resettlement" of the Isle de Jean Charles residents, believe the project will be a precedent for other regions and communities across the world addressing vanishing land and questions of relocation. The resettlement plan could fulfill the desire of a community interested in starting over, one willingly and consciously leaving behind the land of its heritage and culture. Yet the community that the plan is designed for has a different mindset, expressed by Hilton Chaisson, a lifelong resident: "I've lived my whole life here, and I'm going to die here."[16]

To stay requires conventional practices of land ownership and management that promote an existence isolated from ecological networks—to be questioned, discarded, or translated into a new amphibious framework. Architecture must develop amphibious strategies through a new language of *wetness, buoyancy, fluidity, tethering, anchorage,* and *suspension.* Left behind are preconceived notions of environmental *control, protection, resistance,* and *permanence.* This new agenda rejects resilience—understood here as the effort to protect existing endangered settlements through the management or control of ecological contexts—and instead adopts a sophisticated symbiotic existence, adapting and evolving within a dynamic and fluid environment.

[14] Coral Davenport and Campbell Robertson, "Resettling the First American 'Climate Refugees,'" *New York Times*, May 3, 2016, http://www.nytimes.com/2016/05/03/us/resettling-the-first-american-climate-refugees.html.

[15] "About the Project," Isle De Jean Charles Resettlement and Survival, accessed August 28, 2017, http://www.coastalresettlement.org/about-the-project.html.

[16] Hilton Chaisson, quoted in Davenport and Robertson, "Resettling the First American 'Climate Refugees.'"

Top, *Land reclamation, facilitated by dredging ships, expands fixed ground laterally;* bottom, *The jack-up barge produces ground opportunistically, abandoning fixity.*

in parallel

a conversation with
Vincent James and Jennifer Yoos

Pamphlet Architecture 36 authors: In your recent book *Parallel Cities* you examine the urban context as a laminated, three-dimensional conglomeration of program, circulation, service and served, public and private, and pedestrian/vehicular patterns over time and space. These forces often revolve around the changing role of infrastructures and cities—and our relationships within them. While conventional planning has typically relied on a planimetric approach to make improvements or address adverse conditions, your research demonstrates the historical importance of the z-axis in urban morphogenesis. Can you speak to the benefits and challenges of this expanded understanding of urban form?

Jennifer Yoos: In the introduction to *Parallel Cities*, we outline an evolution of the street from early settlements, where it was a simple surface that people walked on, to something that has become increasingly complex and three-dimensional in modern cities. As creative space occupiers, humans have always been interested in maximizing their opportunities in three dimensions. But what comes along with that, of course, are questions of cost, capital, and then control. There is an important social aspect to three-dimensional urban space: it typically involves significant capital investments. So the open terrain where you walk, which everyone thinks of as free space in the city, is much more complex when you consider it in three dimensions and then introduce questions of ownership and public access.

Vincent James: Through our research, we have come to recognize that three-dimensional urbanism is something that happens all the time. We would argue that we should avoid becoming so simplistic in how we think about these urban strategies that we ignore both the consequences and the opportunities of three-dimensional urban space. For example, the High Line is generally viewed as a space of leisure in a city that is very busy and congested.

It has also generated a lot of development in its proximity. But what is most important is how it answered a latent need for a place of leisure on the West Side of Manhattan. It unleashed this potential. That's why it was transformative.

JY: But it is also interesting because the High Line was built on an elevated rail line, a preexisting infrastructural fragment. It was a found object that increased pedestrian connectivity and layered in a diversity of urban programs. The different forms of connectivity did not exist when it was functioning solely as an isolated layer. Connecting and disconnecting are two constantly shifting characteristics motivating three-dimensional urbanisms.

VJ: Parallel to that, we have recently been talking about identifying the relative durability of various urban systems. Durable and long-lasting parts of the city like high-rise buildings and infrastructures—or symbolic spaces for that matter—are different from the more temporary urban forms like commercial space and small-scale, street-oriented activities. These want to change, need to change, so they should be considered differently within three-dimensional urban space. So if you start thinking of a city in terms of the durability of its various social and economic aspects, what does that suggest? And how would you then deal with that sectionally? In other words, tall buildings are much more durable than little sheds out in the park or food trucks, right? But there's a kind of chemistry that's possible on the ground level that's not possible on the fiftieth floor. Something else can happen there. If you look at the entire city this way—in section—and set up the key planning principles based on this understanding, you allow for greater plasticity in the areas where it makes the most sense.

PA36: A laminar urbanism suggests a more nuanced understanding of ground: one where there is no assumption of a constant "elevation zero," but instead a potentially rich topographic condition. In other words, *Parallel Cities*

suggests an urban situation in tune with its extant physical and ecological conditions. What responsibility do cities have to these conditions and processes?

JY: Hong Kong is a really interesting case study because its complex topography, which includes reclaimed land, has been used to create new development sites and nodal points connecting to the underground Mass Transit Railway. In Hong Kong infrastructure is deployed to ameliorate specific conditions in new developments. Urban space is being continually created and recombined three-dimensionally. Singapore is another city that is blurring the lines between the natural and the built in terms of how it integrates green space and position programs in multilevel urban space. This is partly because they have such limited land resources. But in Singapore there is also a more synthetic attitude about the city.

PA36: In terms of resources, does the city recognize that the boundary of its system is much greater than the city limits, so that the territory that might belong to the city is orders of magnitude larger than the city itself? Do cities need to start looking internally to generate feeding systems for their ambitions, be they for the economy, leisure, or something else?

JY: The "island" city-state is an interesting model. You see it being revisited now in London's financial district, which is competing with global cities like Dubai to get companies to relocate and invest there. There are tax incentives and other economic benefits, but they are also trying to create a certain quality of life to attract people, by introducing green space and new transportation infrastructure while also producing a certain appearance of stability. But this also includes speculative developments like residential towers that can stand empty because they are intended principally as investment vehicles for outside capital. They are not necessarily conceived in relation to the local economy per se but are speculations based on their potential to attract and concentrate capital. So these "global cities," as Saskia Sassen pointed out, are always dependent on much wider economic territories.

VJ: You could ask, how does a locality actually come to terms with its Sloterdijkian exterior, right? As well as with its larger context? Its environmental context? From our view, forces that increase density and complexity within a circumscribed territory have an inherent tendency toward three-dimensional urban space—often simply for the spectacle. And then these forms are always conditional, based on social structures, economics, and class. So the three-dimensional city should never be considered as a simple entity. The city is made up of multiple social entities simultaneously occupying and articulating the same three-dimensional space in innumerable ways. Our analysis of the multilevel city made this very clear to us. Defining those articulations is a question of power and politics.

PA36: Looking at environmental conditions as they engage the city, we are finding this is a much larger question, not necessarily rooted in architecture. These relationships have implications for landscape and urban planning, and that makes them even more complex. Where does our role within the discipline fall?

JY: This is the question of landscape urbanism—of dissolving disciplinary boundaries until the way that you think of what architecture is and what it is concerned with starts to shift. We advocate dissolving these boundaries. They aren't a productive way to address contemporary problems.

VJ: Looking at multilevel urbanisms, we were forced to confront many of these questions—issues that surround architecture or are embedded and ignored.

William R. Leigh, "Great City of the Future," Cosmopolitan, November, 1908. Leigh's elaborate portrayal of vertically stratified infrastructural layers foreshadows a future need to confront a new understanding of ground.

JY: Although I should add that we are not teaching urbanism per se. We teach architectural studios and try to open them up to urban issues. A lot of what we are talking about is at an architectural scale: how do you think about circulation, program, and the integration of all of these things? That thinking can happen at a smaller scale in the city, but it is of course always situated within a larger context.

PA36: We understand the city as an accumulation of small and incremental changes, where architectural or landscape decisions create aggregated change. Within this timeline, there are also large shifts, moments of top-down impositions. How do these influences negotiate the city?

JY: We talk a lot about the shift between planning and nonplanning. From a planning perspective there is often a desire to come up with a complete solution, and this can be problematic. On the other hand, there are process-oriented strategies, like those that began with Team 10, which operate in a more piecemeal way. This is why we started to become really interested in the early MARS Group[1] in Britain. They were thinking about how you adapt to existing conditions and then over time end up with a completely different condition. Organic development is such an important process, but it is difficult to implement it purposefully at a large scale. Rem Koolhaas discusses this in his *Project Japan: Metabolism Talks.* In many cases the Metabolists achieved the appearance of an organic process formally but not in reality. Nevertheless, their ideas are still important.

VJ: Exactly. We are interested in tensions between scales of implementation or modification, but also how those ideas are represented. There is master planning—like we see with Le Corbusier, CIAM, and other top-down strategies. And then there is the iconic imagery of someone like Ludwig Hilberseimer. Many of the movements that emerged in the midsixties

Regional Plan Association, Movement Systems Analysis Model (detail), Urban Design Manhattan, 1969. The exposed layers of the city's movement infrastructure reveal patterns for both the traversal and occupation of a laminar urbanism.

suggested a more granular strategy for urban implementation and infrastructure. It's a question of intent.

We find the political questions involved in infrastructure fascinating. Who will build it? Who will fund it? Can it be sustained in the future? What does it do for the urban experience, and what are the broader consequences? These are really political and economic questions that have an enormous impact on the environment and society.

PA36: Then how do we interact with it? And who inhabits it? And what does it represent?

JY: I mean, part of our fascination with ideal or absolute urban models, and with images of the city, is how they actually enter the real world and evolve with urban processes. As they spread, they mutate. In the discipline of architecture, we rarely trace the trajectory of an idea across styles and periods, or from ideal to real. What was interesting to us was the mix of these things. How something develops within a design profession to accomplish one thing and is then appropriated for something completely different. When you take an urban model that has developed over time and has all these layers—the social, the service, the infrastructural—and you displace it with something where the impact is not fully understood, you see the unintended consequences of things that happen quickly, often at a large scale.

PA36: The question of agenda is interesting because it tends to be divorced from what the actual consequences are. For example, the Army Corps of Engineers intended to control the flow of the Mississippi River to sustain economic growth. And then it trickles into the locations of urban developments, has cultural influences, and produces a massive ecological shift. You get saltwater moving further up the river, which changes the character of the environment and relocates certain natural resources.

VJ: We believe that urban morphogenesis is a metabolic process. But it is subject to all of those natural forces and the consequences of earlier actions. Nothing exists without a context or a history. What we think we need or want or fantasize about is usually very limiting and quite often does not account for the flux of real conditions and natural forces. Traditional settlement practices evolved over time, so there was a feedback loop that informed their evolution, but even these forms were vulnerable to environmental change. And currently environmental change is accelerating.

JY: Yes. And due to this constant shift in agendas, all the time, how do you actually sustain a concept of public space or a larger scale urban concept through these transformations? Three-dimensional urbanism really complicates these issues.

PA36: It's an urban or territorial idea, but agendas are ultimately just ambitions. If decisions were made through the lens of consequence rather than the lens of ambition, and by playing out possible outcomes in a different way, the results might be different. Can you speak to infrastructure's role in the development of urbanism—at times an afterthought, at others a leader—and how you see that role changing in future cities?

VJ: Henri Lefebvre and others criticized the overly rational, machinelike concept of the modernist city. We agree with this criticism, so we are interested in how the spaces of connection and flow that are typically infrastructural become social spaces. In our design for the Weisman Plaza competition we worked with the Washington Avenue Bridge, which spans the Mississippi River, to connect the east- and west-bank campuses of the University of Minnesota.[2] The original infrastructure was conceived in utilitarian terms as a singular and isolated transportation conduit for cars, buses, and pedestrians.

JY: But we wanted to bring out its latent potential as public space so we cross-programmed and connected it with a variety of new spaces for social events and other leisure activities. We wanted to get beyond the destination planning that often saps the pleasures of urban life from much of our daily experience. We believe that designers and planners have to take care to reconcile the utilitarian agenda with the need for pleasure and sociability in cities—especially with infrastructure where it is often sacrificed. One interesting question is, who defines infrastructure? There are very specific definitions, or categories, that dictate what infrastructure is for and who pays for it. If it's connected to highway transportation, it is conceived one way. If it's about flood control, it does something else. But this list of individual functional objectives limits the quality of our urban environments. In order to succeed in enriching the urban experience, we need to think about multiple objectives. No aspect of the urban environment should be conceived reductively.

We would say that the design disciplines have the tendency to work against this complex urban unity. Architecture often does. Landscape often does too. But the urban environment cannot be broken down into disciplinary fields. Infrastructure is often left unconsidered because it does not feed disciplinary interests and because of its role as the often unloved matrix connecting discrete cultural events. One could argue that great cities are measured in large part by the richness of their connective layers.

PA36: You have previously written on the topic of social engineering, calling on architects to understand our role in the generation and structuring of social space. You advise a calculated participation between utopian desires and a "reciprocal fate in the service of ruthless commercial interests," and speak to the importance of an awareness of our agency.[3] Are architects also ecological engineers?

JY: We used the term *social engineering* provocatively, because it is seen in such a negative light, as an authoritarian concept. But the reality is that the spaces we make all have an impact on social interaction, either positively or negatively. So while we focus on experience and aesthetics, we need to remain aware of how our designs affect people as social beings.

VJ: We use the term *social engineering* as a form of self-reflexivity. It is a tool to help us think more broadly about what we are doing as architects. It is about our sense of responsibility, not our authority.

PA36: Right. A design process does not begin with solutions, but it should instead identify the right questions; an understanding of resources and ecological systems plays an increasingly important role in this dialogue. Through design agency, can we begin to question ecological decisions and consequences? And with this understanding of consequence, what responsibility does design have?

VJ: We advocate for what we call a "reflexive practice" because so often the most important obstacle to addressing a problem is self-generated ignorance. If your discipline or your area of interest allows you to ignore the consequences of what you're doing, it is very difficult to break out of those practices. But since the environment is changing so rapidly, flexible thinking is more important than ever. If there were a single thing to program into our design thinking, it would be adaptability.

JY: We have experimented with this in past projects. As part of a design competition many years ago, we speculated on a kind of nodal version of what we see now as multilevel urbanism. It made sense to us, looking at our own system in Minneapolis, that it wouldn't be homogeneously connected but would instead be adapted to different contexts, with level-to-level interactions playing out, as in Cedric Price's Fun Palace (1961, unbuilt). But these interventions can self-replicate under certain circumstances and generate a larger system very quickly. The idea that you create something temporal that then becomes the catalyst for changing the context around it is fascinating, but the consequences can be either good or bad. Let's say that multilevel urbanisms are employed in coastal cities in response to rising sea levels. There are many scenarios that might be played out as possible responses. It would be as if the ground plane was being reinvented through architecture, infrastructure, and landscape. That could happen in many ways and on many planes. Each decision might affect the whole and could change the entire urban system.

PA36: The United States, in particular, has been criticized for designing twenty- or fifteen-year buildings. But could that be an effective strategy if the building responds architecturally and is built with the foresight that it will go away? The idea that the building has a cycle that's shorter may allow the context to adapt and the building to be less detrimental.

JY: Right, and we necessarily do these short-term buildings because of the economic growth cycle, which isn't looking for the better urban outcome. And I think the model that we're talking about isn't about the economic benefit of providing a better urban outcome; it's about the fact that you're designing the city, or infrastructure, with a more long-term agenda, not just a short-term payback.

PA36: Maybe the architecture exists within a short-term economic model, but in a strategic way also exists within a system of assessment, which has a longer life span, striving for a more ambitious end goal. It's a shift in thinking about what a building actually is.

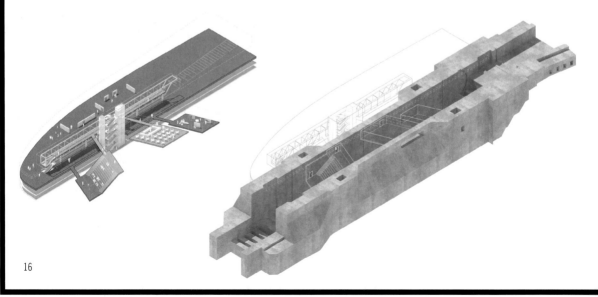

VJ: We find Bruno Latour's actor-network theory very useful, even profound, for thinking about the way that objects and events—architecture, for example—become integrated urbanistically as part of a much larger field of actors. As architects, we have to make these connections if we want to be part of the urban environment, part of the landscape, part of the ecological systems, and to respond to larger climatic forces. These are all bigger than the narrowly circumscribed idea of the architect.

JY: Yes, exactly. The building is not the point of the exercise. It's a participant in it.

VJ: By the way, that is the opposite of the neoliberal architectural model, which radicalized and isolated the individual architect. The idea of the participant may be a shift, and it is so refreshing to see something that's not about projects in isolation but actually the aggregate effects of many little projects. Latour advocates for greater and greater sensitivity. These connections are the only way to achieve the adaptability necessary for our times.

PA36: If we take the idea that a building or infrastructure can act as a catalyst that understands a fifty- or hundred-year future, how can the precedents and conceptual framework established around the "synthesized city" be deployed to address the problem of sea-level rise that is predicted in that time frame? Given a dynamic site, which is land now but in the future will be aquatic, can it be reprogrammed to exist in an amphibious manner?

JY: One can imagine multilevel urban forms that respond to rising sea levels or interlaced building masses hovering above tidal marshes or rafts of gently undulating residential communities. One can also imagine cities huddled against dark seawalls that are periodically submerged and pumping frantically to stay dry. We conclude *Parallel Cities* by citing Anthony Vidler's work on utopia and his attempt to revive the use of ideal urban models as "tools for thinking."[4] One of the most important things we can do now is to explore these possible futures. But this carries with it an obligation to maintain a critical relationship with our ideas so that they do not blind us to how they interact with other realities. This is the reflexivity we talked about.

VJ: There is a paradox here. Along with the optimism of utopian thinking, we also need to imagine how the same forms of urbanism may generate a dystopia. Since we are imagining our future in uncertain times, we must conceive our new cities with conviction and yet keep them at arm's length so our ideas do not beguile us. Ultimately, we are advocating that we dream of ideal cities without the delirium of sleep.

Vincent James, FAIA, and Jennifer Yoos, FAIA, are principals of VJAA and coauthors of Parallel Cities: The Multilevel Metropolis.

[1] The Modern Architectural Research (MARS) Group was the English branch of the International Congresses of Modern Architecture (CIAM), known for their speculations on interwar and postwar development in London.

[2] VJAA was selected as the winner of the Mississippi River Bridge Plaza Design Competition. The site is adjacent to the newly expanded Weisman Art Museum on the University of Minnesota's campus.

[3] James, Vincent, and Jennifer Yoos. *VJAA: Vincent James Associates Architects.* Princeton Architectural Press, 2007. 125.

[4] Anthony Vidler, "How to Invent Utopia: The Fortunes and Misfortunes of Plato's Polis," Mellon lecture at the Canadian Centre for Architecture, May 17, 2005. Via Yoos, Jennifer, Vincent James, and Andrew Blauvelt. *Parallel Cities: The Multilevel Metropolis.* Minneapolis: Walker Art Center, 2016.

The Falls by VJAA, in progress, Minneapolis, MN. The project occupies spaces adjacent to and within a permanently decommissioned lock. A variety of observation points allow for unique sectional relationships to the water around and inside the lock as it rises and falls seasonally.

I. WAITING TO LEAVE

Whether to leave is only the first of the hard questions: Where does everyone go? What claim do they have to what is left behind? Will they be welcomed by their new neighbors? Will there be work nearby? Who will be allowed to join them?
—*Coral Davenport and Campbell Robertson, "Resettling the First American 'Climate Refugees,'"* New York Times, *May 3, 2016*

To prepare to leave is a mobilization toward mobility. The questions set forth by Davenport and Robertson, quoted above, expose the difficult task of relocation, even at the scale of a single community. Expanding the scope of resettlement to a territorial, or even global, scale seems impossible. Yet the development of large-scale temporary settlements and associated infrastructures is inevitable and necessary. Global mapping demonstrates that over 600 million people live in low-lying elevations threatened by sea-level rise. While many of these people can access higher ground farther inland, other populations will soon be forced to face these questions. Island nations in Melanesia, Micronesia, Polynesia, and the Maldives are particularly susceptible.

Morphing Edges

As glaciers melt and water levels rise globally, the transformation is largely absorbed along edge conditions. The solid black portions depict the future morphed edges, or the slow and gradual process of transformation along the edges where water meets dry land. The reduced continental footprints, defined by the interior of the black transformation zone, abstract a future timeline of submerged land. Varying predictions suggest these water levels in the twenty-second century; how will the existing edge populations and settlements transition to an aquatic life?

The accompanying timeline, the first of four presented alongside the introduction to each section, charts the sea level over the past thousands of years. As the sections progress, the timeline focuses on more recent histories and compares the earth's geological changes to global human populations.

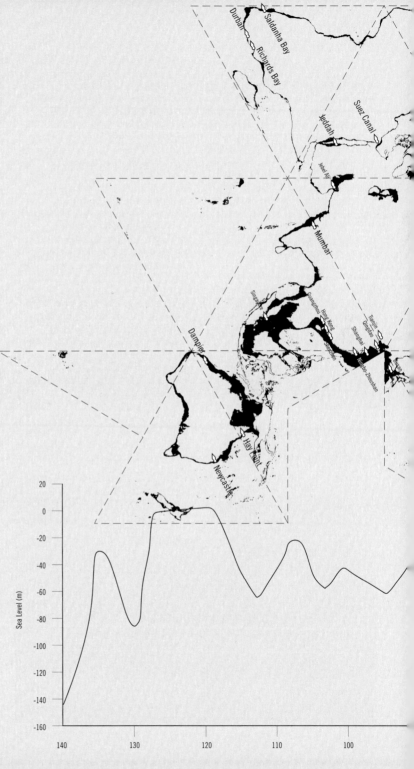

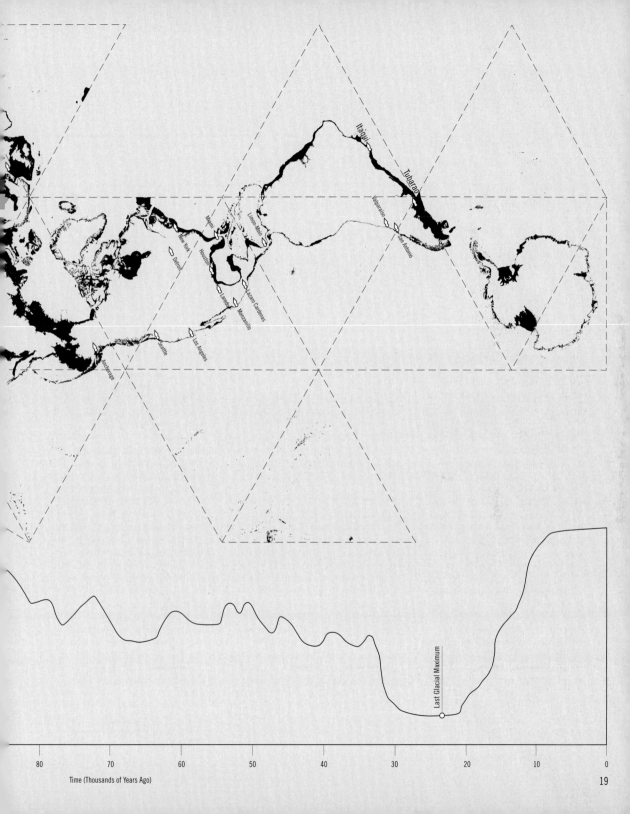

Itaqui

Tubarão

Valparaíso

San Antonio

Miami

New York

Detroit

Houston

Limon-Moin

Laredo

Lazaro Cardenas

Manzanillo

Seattle

Los Angeles

Anchorage

Last Glacial Maximum

Time (Thousands of Years Ago)

80   70   60   50   40   30   20   10   0

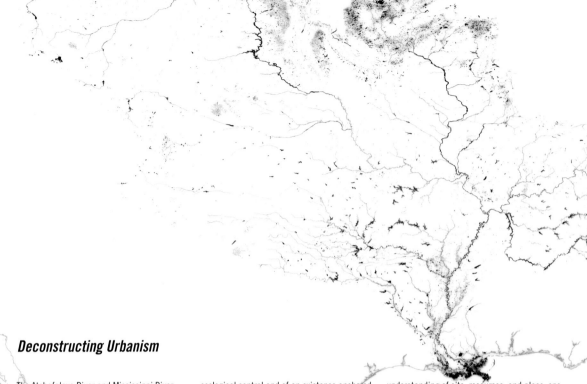

Deconstructing Urbanism

The Atchafalaya River and Mississippi River Delta comprise one territory facing inexorable change. Rooted in habit and implemented in practice is an intricate web of river adaptations, built levees, earthen mounds, outlets, inlets, man-made cuts, bayou remnants, canals, and pump stations—all created with the goal of controlling the environment for the benefit of human settlement and expansion. The agenda of control was set forth centuries ago by European settlers, reinforced over the decades by the US Army and federal government, and cemented with the establishment of the Army Corps of Engineers.[1]

The implementation of man-made control mechanisms—pseudonatural lakes, channels, the Intracoastal Waterway, and the Wax Lake outlet exist as human-constructed remnants scarring the region.[2] The continuous construction and reconstruction of these control mechanisms, as well as the ever increasing allocation of assets for resource extraction and constant water-level rise resulting in land loss, raise questions about whether historic methods can satisfy contemporary needs. The Atchafalaya River and Mississippi River Delta territory, as a place of study, offers an opportunity to interrogate the probable failure of

ecological control and of an existence anchored in place. The disruption caused by these forces suggests the possibility that delta settlements may need to be abruptly abandoned in the not-too-distant future. Projective strategies can work to reframe the trajectory of engagement within residence, industry, and recreation.

While the history of human settlement includes multiple precedents of urban decommissioning, this choice to divest commitment in maintaining a city cannot be categorized as an active urbanistic agenda. Departure can be spurred by a range of issues: economic collapse (Detroit, Michigan), catastrophic infrastructure failure (Chernobyl and Pripyat, Ukrainian SSR), resource depletion (Hashima Island, Japan), pollution (Times Beach, Missouri), political unrest (Craco, Italy), and the effects of war (Hiroshima and Nagasaki, Japan) represent a select few. All these are reactionary instances of decommissioning. A preemptive agenda, by contrast, acknowledges evolving environmental forces and advocates for retreat, abandoning the land once considered home to settle elsewhere. From humankind's history of abandoned cities arises a projective question: do we possess the fortitude to deconstruct cities for the benefit of ecological agendas? A renewed

understanding of site, resources, and place, one that opposes human-centric thinking, presents a flexible new agenda for the city.

Evaluating the worth of a city, and its viability in comparison to its environmental consequence, will always be a difficult process. Determining how to quantify history, culture, time, and embodied energy will expose rifts in human measures of value. When a city becomes unviable as a place of sustained inhabitation—whether due to economic instability, cultural conditions, ecological crisis, political unrest, war, or environmental pressures—a society will be forced to consider its commitment to sustaining it. Decommissioning a city is one possible route toward reconciliation.

A city can be described as layers of infrastructural systems, buildings, and the filigree of human artifice. Embedded in the bricks and mortar of a city is an accumulation of value that can take many forms, both tangible and intangible: energy, time, emotion, culture, history, resources, materials, and potentials. Projections of shifting environmental conditions, climatic forces, and flows of resource networks will position humankind

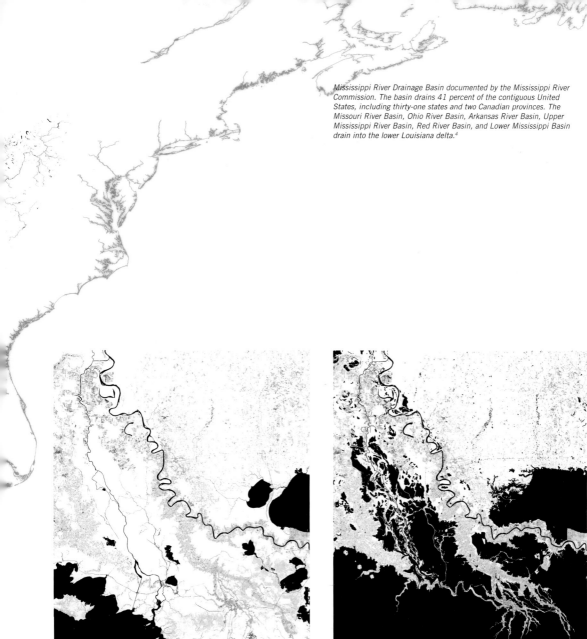

Mississippi River Drainage Basin documented by the Mississippi River Commission. The basin drains 41 percent of the contiguous United States, including thirty-one states and two Canadian provinces. The Missouri River Basin, Ohio River Basin, Arkansas River Basin, Upper Mississippi River Basin, Red River Basin, and Lower Mississippi Basin drain into the lower Louisiana delta.[4]

The Mississippi River Delta is a complex mélange of land and water constrained by an equally complex series of man-made control mechanisms devised by the Mississippi River Commission (MRC) and implemented through the Flood Control Act of 1928 and the Mississippi River and Tributaries Project.[3] The charge of the MRC is twofold: to control river flooding and to manage economic and property interests through the restriction of river-channel migration.

Extent of inundation of delta floodplains with the current flood control mechanisms in place. Examined at this scale, flood control can be understood to provide only a false sense of security.

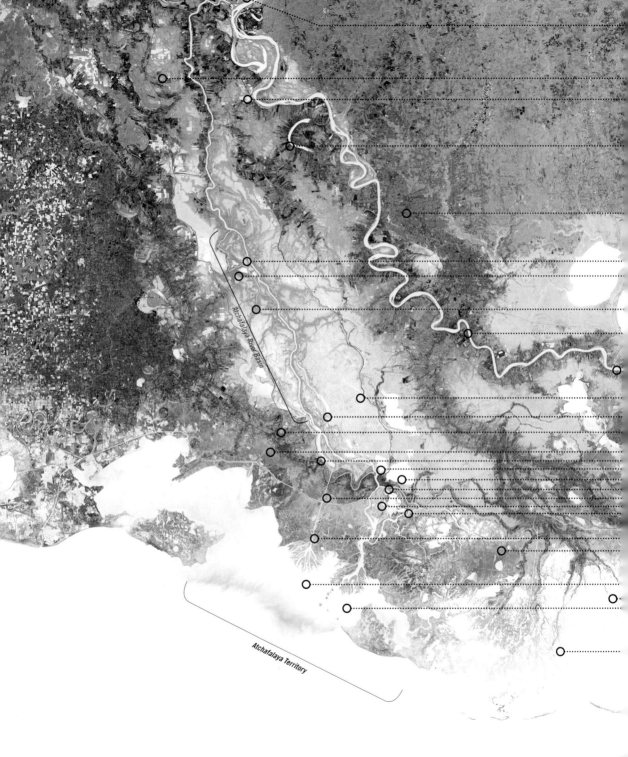

Atchafalaya River Basin

Atchafalaya Territory

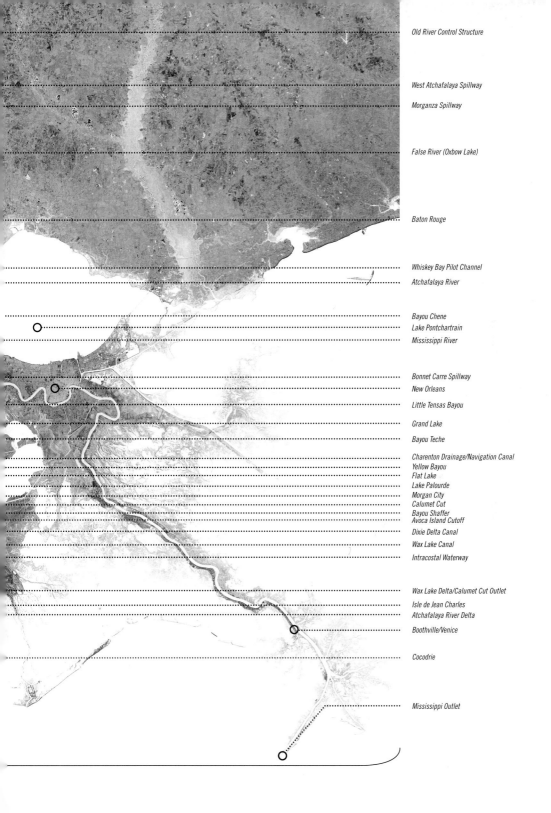

Old River Control Structure

West Atchafalaya Spillway

Morganza Spillway

False River (Oxbow Lake)

Baton Rouge

Whiskey Bay Pilot Channel
Atchafalaya River

Bayou Chene
Lake Pontchartrain
Mississippi River

Bonnet Carre Spillway
New Orleans

Little Tensas Bayou

Grand Lake

Bayou Teche

Charenton Drainage/Navigation Canal
Yellow Bayou
Flat Lake
Lake Palourde
Morgan City
Calumet Cut
Bayou Shaffer
Avoca Island Cutoff
Dixie Delta Canal
Wax Lake Canal
Intracostal Waterway

Wax Lake Delta/Calumet Cut Outlet
Isle de Jean Charles
Atchafalaya River Delta
Boothville/Venice

Cocodrie

Mississippi Outlet

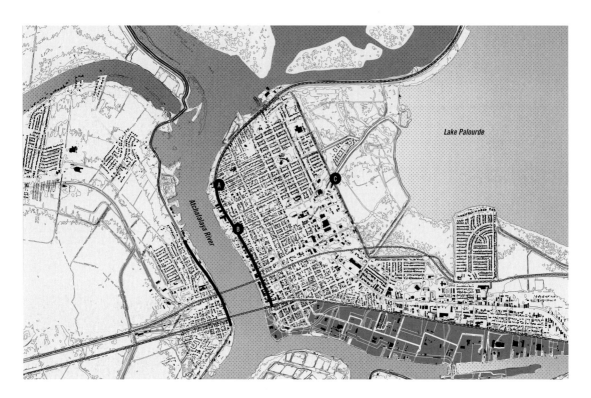

Lake Palourde

Atchafalaya River

Twenty-First Century Morgan City

Morgan City is effectively an island dividing the Atchafalaya River to the west from Lake Palourde to the east. Mapping the forces and flows that surround Morgan City reveals the fragility of settlements in the delta. The controlled evolution of the Mississippi and Atchafalaya River Deltas demonstrates the extent to which Morgan City's existence depends on water-control mechanisms: earthen levees, seawalls, floodgates, dredging, man-made channels, and powered pump stations. Yet these infrastructures of control are a guise. They represent security of place in concept, but in practice are no match for the power of thousands of gallons of muddy water rushing through the Atchafalaya River, fed from the mighty Mississippi and the rising water of Lake Palourde. The communities within the delta will soon face the question, can static cities continue to persist in this fluid and dynamic environment?

to rethink its urbanism. Urban change in the Anthropocene has principally consisted of growth and expansion. But what about abandonment?

What does the decommissioning of a city look like? Can the interpretation of a city transcend terra firma and find stable adaptation? Morgan City, Louisiana—adjacent to the Atchafalaya River, Flat Lake, and Lake Palourde—offers a precedent for analyzing the provocation of urban decommissioning. The city must constantly monitor and tend to its surroundings: the Atchafalaya River yearns to slowly and steadily migrate east and west across the delta, regardless of human settlement patterns, while the settlement of Morgan City is defined by

static territorial limits. The binding of the urban settlement to the river for economic means, human sustenance, and resource transportation and extraction raises a number of questions: Can urbanism be conceived as a kinetic entity in opposition to a static being? What methods could the city use to move in tandem with the river's constant channel migration across time and space? As the river is forced, by human means, to follow a fixed path, the terra firma within the delta rapidly erodes, consuming vegetation, altering the saline content of the ecological system, and irreversibly redefining the ecology of lower Louisiana. Thus, Morgan City embodies a contradiction: the resources that support the city are being eroded by its very existence. Is Morgan City worth the effort?

This series of images provide a glimpse into the history of Morgan City. The adjacent Atchafalaya River fostered prosperity in the form of trade, oil industry, and shrimping in the eighteenth and nineteenth centuries. Yet the Atchafalaya frequently flooded the town, disrupting typical daily activities and economic exchange. Images of the floods of 1912 and 1927 provide examples of the residents' adaptability to changing water levels.

A. *Levee Road and Front Street, looking to Atchafalaya*

B. *Front Street and Terrebonne Street, looking to Atchafalaya*

C. *Marguerite Street and Veterans Boulevard Pump Station—In*

A. *Levee Road and Front Street, looking to Morgan City*

B. *Front Street and Terrebonne Street, looking to Morgan City*

C. *Marguerite Street and Veterans Boulevard Pump Station—Out*

The Mississippi River flood of 1973 compromised the newly constructed floodgate system, the Old River Control Structure (ORCS), and uncovered the inevitable: everything constructed has an expiration date. The acknowledgment of ORCS's eventual expiration provides a platform to rethink humans' involvement in shaping the Atchafalaya River, the Mississippi River, and their conjoined delta. Phasing out the ORCS in order to return the territory to its original river networks will allow the Atchafalaya River and the Mississippi River to flow and wander freely toward the Gulf of Mexico. Current conditions confine the river network through several static urban settlements and prevent the natural migration of the river channel. The perseverance of the inhabitants within the delta should not go unnoticed; however, the naïveté that humankind displays in its belief in the controllability of the Atchafalaya River sets the stage for the catastrophic decimation of settlements in and around the river. With sea-level rise, the Atchafalaya River, Flat Lake, Lake Palourde, and Bayou Shaffer surrounding Morgan City place the city below surrounding water level on all sides and reinforces the "bathtubbing" of the city through tall protective levee walls. How can the slow, staged decommissioning of the ORCS, the deconstruction of the city, the displacement of inhabitants, and the relocation of materials and resources interpolate a positive dialogue between humankind and nature to shape a new agenda for urbanism?

[1] "The U.S. Army Corps of Engineers: A Brief History; The Beginnings to 1815," US Army Corps of Engineers, accessed June 4, 2017, http://www.usace.army.mil/about/history/brief-history-of-the-corps/beginnings.

[2] Adam Voiland, "Growing Deltas in Atchafalaya Bay," NASA Earth Observatory, November 7, 1984, https://earthobservatory.nasa.gov/Features/WorldOfChange/wax_lake.php.

[3] "Mississippi River and Tributaries Project," US Army Corps of Engineers Mississippi Valley Division, accessed July 5, 2017, http://www.mvd.usace.army.mil/About/Mississippi-River-Commission-MRC/Mississippi-River-Tributaries-Project-MR-T.

[4] Rep. No. Mississippi River Commission 41-1 at 41-105 (2007). Report of the Secretary of the Army on Civil Works Activities for FY 2007.

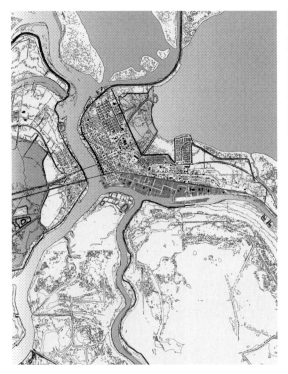

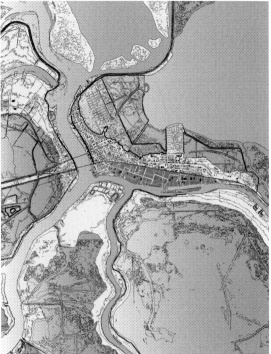

Phase I: Post–Industrial Revolution Desettlement

Increased investment in flood-control mechanisms and environmental-management strategies have defined the philosophy of delta settlement since the early nineteenth century. However, a juxtaposing framework of rising water and ecological crisis suggests a divestment in man-made protection interventions, and even the decommissioning of the city. This map sets forth the first step toward the recomposition of Morgan City to allow water to flow where buildings once stood. The low-lying regions of Morgan City are decommissioned first. It is critical to understand that decommissioning will require construction. As portions of Morgan City are dismantled, the reconfiguration of residences, commercial interests, institutions, and governmental facilities to sit on a compact footprint will require short-term architectural solutions that also coordinate timeline, capital investments, and embodied energy.

In Phase I, control systems are dismantled and a fluid transitional zone, defined by fluctuating water levels and changing pockets of terra firma, is allowed to take shape. Programmatically, the city's permanent and private settlement zones will be transformed into fluid, transitional public spaces, adaptable to evolving forms of recreational activity within the delta. Resources are allowed to flourish within this zone, suggesting a "new natural" within the anthropocentric ecology.

Phase II: Dismantling Management

As the footprint of the urban fabric contracts, traces of the city's origins begin to surface. The strategies of decommissioning are committed to active participation in the networks of resource extraction, manipulation, and distribution that are vital to Morgan City, particularly the petroleum and shrimping industries. Commercial, institutional, governmental, and residential interests will migrate toward the western and northern edges of the industrial region.

Phase II proposes the continued dismantling of the various control mechanisms within and around Morgan City, allowing low-lying areas to absorb sea-level rise at a slow and steady pace. Simultaneously, the constructed levees to the west of the city continue to guide the Atchafalaya River south to the Gulf of Mexico, providing a buffer for the inhabited areas on higher ground at moments when the Atchafalaya River swells.

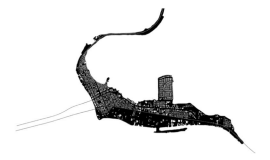

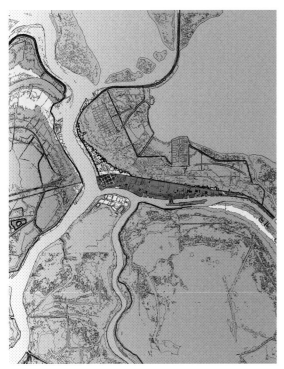

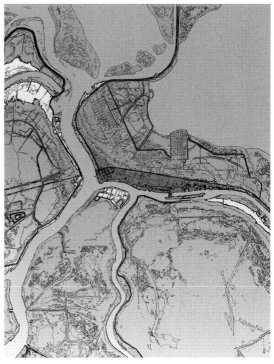

Phase III: Contracted Living

The final throes of Morgan City's desettlement: flood-control mechanisms, intermodal systems, networks of levees, sea walls, Louisiana Highway 182, US Route 90, and the BNSF and Union Pacific railways are decommissioned. The remaining portion of Morgan City becomes the southernmost section of Saint Mary Parish, accessible by Louisiana Highway 70 from the north. The decommissioning of Morgan City ultimately uncovers the difficult conversation that the delta and coastal communities will need to begin in the coming years: as the material city leaves, so too does its culture of place. The strategy to consciously decommission situates humankind as an active participant in the abandonment of human settlements in the delta. Can humankind learn to let go?

Phase III provides a framework for breaking habits. Morgan City is now almost unrecognizable in form and function from the twenty-first century methods of permanence in place, static habitats, and transportation infrastructure. In this future, transportation networks exist solely as aquatic movement patterns, and occupation of the city is temporal—focused on the needs of resource and industry supported by flexible and kinetic "residence hubs."

Phase IV: Port Docking

Sea-level rise, increased storm severity and frequency, and evolving delta flow patterns intensify daily habitation within the delta region. Traces of settlements mark a now distant post–Industrial Revolution era. The idea of control has eroded; in its place, an integrated dialogue of humankind and nature is found. The delta is littered with the markings of obsolete levee walls, now transformed into docking stations and cultural markers.

Phase IV suggests a concept of place found through a kinetic existence—one that acknowledges change and supports a focused experience of site. Industry remains; permanent settlements are gone. Infrastructures are decommissioned or adapted to an aquatic environment. Leisure also remains, building on historical traditions of interaction with the delta's flora and fauna.

Shipbreakers

Urbanization is a process of reconstitution—from raw ore to shaped steel to assembled structure, carried in deadweight tons from sites of extraction to zones of inhabitation. Very large ore carriers (VLOCs), owned by multinational corporations susceptible to global economic fluctuations, handle the seaborne movement of ore and, implicitly, the global potential for physical growth along with it. For example, a torrent of orders for new vessels in the mid-2000s economic upturn led to a peak in global seaborne ore capacity in 2012, but in the years after the 2008 recession, maintenance of those ships became unsustainable, leading to a precipitous drop in ore capacity that lasted through 2015.[1]

The statistical expression of "lost deadweight tonnage" is materially manifested at the southern edge of Bangladesh, on the outskirts of Chittagong, where the thriving yet controversial practice of shipbreaking takes place. Here cargo ships, oil tankers, and bulk carriers are run close to shore during high tide and beached, left to be taken apart and sold for scrap. The rusting steel hulls that remain along the waterfront dwarf the coastal communities living in their shadows; the beached vessels have become the skyline of the city.

Chittagong maintains a precarious relationship with the sea. While the vessels along its shore represent a latent economic opportunity embedded in the global transportation network, rising waters threaten these low-lying spaces along the Bay of Bengal. The local and migrant populations that comprise the shipbreaking working class take on the perilous job of dismantling and cutting apart the hulking steel beasts that ceaselessly come to rest on their beaches. Yet as this population will inevitably be forced to search for higher ground with sea-level rise, the vessels that find their way to Chittagong could offer another sort of opportunity.

The largest VLOCs reach 65 meters in breadth, 362 meters in length, and rise approximately 46 meters high from the surface of the beach, exceeding most Manhattan blocks in area and volume.[2]

Manhattan Block
Length: 246m
Width: 60m

Vale Brasil
Length: 362m
Width: 65m

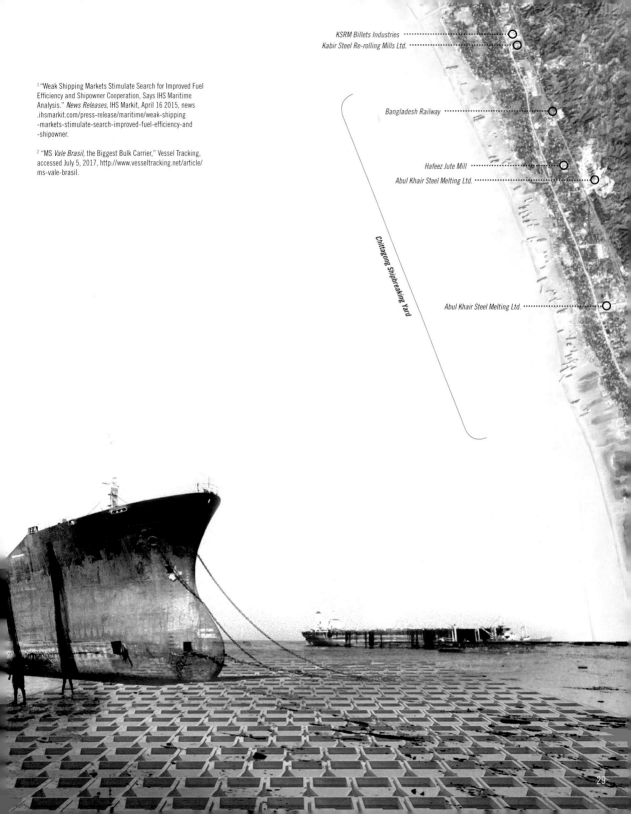

[1] "Weak Shipping Markets Stimulate Search for Improved Fuel Efficiency and Shipowner Cooperation, Says IHS Maritime Analysis." *News Releases*, IHS Markit, April 16 2015, news.ihsmarkit.com/press-release/maritime/weak-shipping-markets-stimulate-search-improved-fuel-efficiency-and-shipowner.

[2] "MS *Vale Brasil*, the Biggest Bulk Carrier," Vessel Tracking, accessed July 5, 2017, http://www.vesseltracking.net/article/ms-vale-brasil.

KSRM Billets Industries

Kabir Steel Re-rolling Mills Ltd.

Bangladesh Railway

Hafeez Jute Mill

Abul Khair Steel Melting Ltd.

Chittagong Shipbreaking Yard

Abul Khair Steel Melting Ltd.

The solution to resettlement will need to be a multipoint strategy, but the vessels offer the inhabitants of Chittagong one opportunity to imagine resettlement. The access to beached ships, coupled with the embedded knowledge of their construction and the art of shipbreaking, will allow the inhabitants of Chittagong to rethink the notion of resettlement. In opposition to completely dismantling the vessels, crews of workers could selectively deconstruct their decks, superstructures, and hulls, offering a tabula rasa upon which to construct communities for harboring the displaced and transporting them to new settlements elsewhere.

In this circumstance, architecture must address the basic need for shelter from harsh environmental conditions, facilitate access to food, and assist in the gathering and production of fresh water for drinking. The best means of accomplishing this is to accept the forces of water and to establish a confrontational proximity to it: an amphibious architecture.

Bangladesh's proximity to major shipping lanes linking East Asia to the Gulf States, long natural beaches, and relatively high poverty rates (49.1 percent) foster shipbreaking along its shores in Chittagong.

● 7. Chittagong

A ship's draft is the vertical distance between the bottom of its hull and the waterline. In Chittagong, draft marks on a vessel's hull can gauge the rising of the sea, helping inhabitants to know when it is time to depart.

Port(s)	Cargo volume (millions of tons, 2015)
1. Mumbai + JNPT	125.14
2. Colombo	30.9
3. Ennore + Chennai	78.45
4. Visakhapatnam	64.21
5. Paradeep	75.77
6. Kolkata	50.19
7. Chittagong	54.78
8. Port klang	219.79
9. Tanjung pelepas	136.28
10. Singapore	575.85

Filtration Buoyage

The continuous bodies of water connecting the planet's land masses can appear site-less, reinforced by humankind's shallow understanding of what exists below the water's surface. As we travel between continents aboard aquatic vessels and aircrafts, the expansiveness of the water conjures thoughts of endlessness and sameness: each wave the same as the last, the depth of the water almost unfathomable, aquatic life mostly invisible. In actuality, the oceans are a complex, layered milieu, where temperature, penetration of light, currents, bathymetry, and surface-air movements produce local specificities that define place within the seeming placelessness of the ocean.

Residue and consequence left by humanity have found their way into the far reaches of the planet, and the ocean is no exception. Our plastic refuse has made the invisible nuances, subtleties, and specificities of the oceans' characteristics visible. As humankind becomes acutely aware of anthropocentric implications, the reality is nothing short of sobering.

How does discarded waste uncover the ocean as a context that solicits a site-specific understanding? Human excess in the form of plastic has invaded the aquatic setting; the majority of plastics, if not all, degrade over time and break down in the presence of UV exposure, a significant element in the ocean's epipelagic zone. The degradation manifests in microfibers, which fall from the epipelagic zones and into the mesopelagic, where the fibers are distributed by underwater currents across large areas of the ocean.

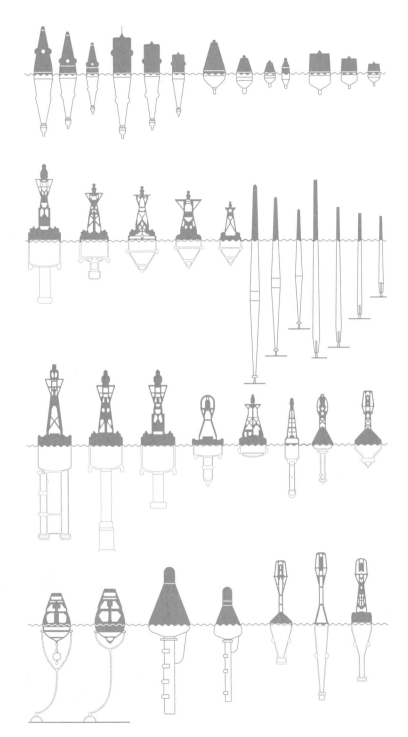

1920 Selected Types of Buoys, US Lighthouse Services

Microfiber Filtration Buoy

Solar array/support framework ....

Removable maintenance cap ....

Colored lens cover, solid state ....
diode with reflective foil and global
positioning system sensor unit

Clean water discharge port ....

Ventricle flow baffles ....

Microfiber filter (removable ....
through upper maintenance cap)

Perforated filter debris cage ....

Water intake channel/intake port ....

Cylinder wall ....

Piston head ....

Filtration buoy carcass (exterior ....
shell)

Connecting rod ....
bump stop and o-ring water seal

Stainless steel set spring ....

Spring seat ....

Large debris screen/water intake ....

Filtration buoy carcass (interior ....
core)

Removable maintenance cap ....
O-ring and water seal ....

Extended connecting rod/cable to ....
anchor

Connection clevis to anchor (or ....
drift sock)

Pollution Identification Buoy

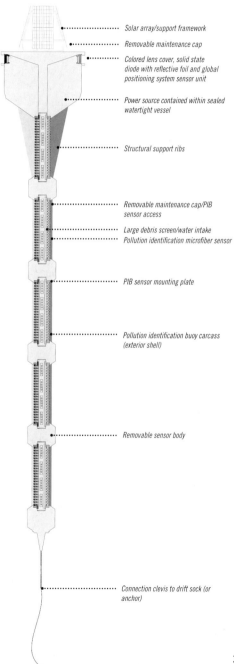

Solar array/support framework ....

Removable maintenance cap ....

Colored lens cover, solid state ....
diode with reflective foil and global
positioning system sensor unit

Power source contained within sealed ....
watertight vessel

Structural support ribs ....

Removable maintenance cap/PIB ....
sensor access

Large debris screen/water intake ....
Pollution identification microfiber sensor ....

PIB sensor mounting plate ....

Pollution identification buoy carcass ....
(exterior shell)

Removable sensor body ....

Connection clevis to drift sock (or ....
anchor)

The filtration buoy aims to extract the ecologically destructive plastic microfibers before they settle to the mesopelagic zone and removal becomes an almost impossible task. A defining characteristic of the ocean—its constant state of motion with relentless persistence—provides the guiding design principles for both filtration and identification buoyage. By harnessing constant motion as a power generator, a pump can create localized flow patterns that move a mixture of water and microfiber through the buoy, where the microfibers can be filtered and contained. The ocean's motion is used as a constant power source for the filtration buoy. The water-intake valve is positioned significantly below the water surface to extract the suspended plastics within the epipelagic zone. In addition, the buoy drifts within the ocean currents, employing environmental forces as its infrastructure manager. The filtration and identification buoy movement pattern choreographed by the ocean current establishes a predictable distribution network able to be overlaid with other ocean current–dependent systems. The buoyage aims to remove plastic from the ocean by uncovering and acknowledging the specificity of place, engaging the embedded knowledge of the global water system.

II. PREPARING TO STAY

Which aspects of home compel people to remain when that home's inundation is inevitable? Is it the material reality of home as a building? The social structures and relationships embedded in the place? The place itself as a hallowed ground?

The choice to stay is born of responsibility, desire, and commitment to preservation—of self and of place. Someday, staying will mean floating. While people may be able to inhabit the same position on the earth, their relationship to water will have to be reconfigured. As coast becomes backshore, backshore becomes foreshore, and foreshore gives way to littoral zone, those choosing to remain must phase in responses to protect what they hold dear. Many communities opting to stay make a choice to endure in spite of the rising water, rather than in cooperation with it. But in order to persist in these places, a new attitude of habitation is necessary.

Absolute Hypsography

Hypsography depicts an absolute understanding of the earth's surface. Admittedly abstract, the continuous representation of bathymetry and contour, (represented as a gradation from dark to light) repositions the z-dimension as a fluid and contiguous ground, effectively eliminating the definitive "edge" between land and water. Through this lens, one reestablishes an understanding of terra firma and aqua firma as a vertically layered, dynamic system; it displaces an accepted idea of them as two abutting horizontal environments. The density within the map represents the accumulation of human settlement; precariously they are often concentrated within littoral zones.

The timeline plots global population growth over hundreds of centuries and provides additional data of global water levels, initiating at the last glacial maximum. The results depict continuous growth among both population and sea water levels. As global population gains increasing density, rising water and dynamic littoral zones have greater effects due to populations concentrated in littoral zones, forcing the question: How do these increasingly populated littoral zones prepare to inhabit their evolving environment?

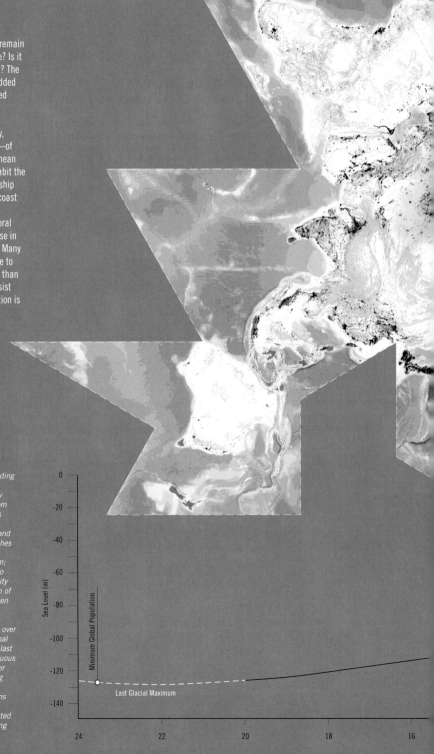

Sea Level (m)

0

-20

-40

-60

-80

-100

-120

-140

Minimum Global Population

Last Glacial Maximum

24   22   20   18   16

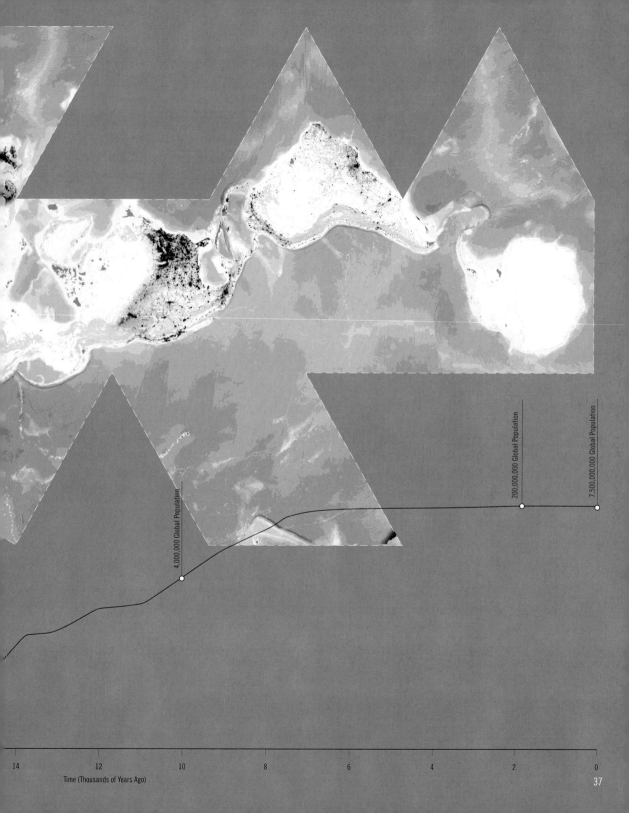

4,000,000 Global Population

200,000,000 Global Population

7,500,000,000 Global Population

14   12   10   8   6   4   2   0

Time (Thousands of Years Ago)

Inhabitable Wave Farm

The Kurumba and Bandos island resorts opened in 1972, together offering a total of 280 beds. Tourism was hardly an industry in the Maldives before then, though you would not get that impression today in Malé, the capital and gateway for the country's 1.2 million annual visitors. Malé itself is home to a permanent population of over 156,000 people, densely packed within 5.8 square kilometers. Looking down from the plane, Malé seems like a region cut from the heart of some anonymous midrise metropolis—its edges characterized by the same density of urban life and pastel-painted concrete as its center, with only a thin necklace of harbored sailboats and dhonis distinguishing its perimeter.

Between 1972 and today, Malé has struggled to grow at a pace equal to the influx of tourism to the country's 1,192 islands—a consequence of political upheaval, geographic isolation, and the rapid rise of its popularity as a tourist destination. Today it is home to a third of the country's population. In a sense, the quality of land of the Maldives conflicts with its quantity, generating an urbanism that expands by means of island hopping. Through land reclamation campaigns from 1979 to 1992, and through ongoing densification within that available landmass, the city of Malé has exceeded the island's physical capacity and has expanded onto its adjacent islands. Land reclamation efforts on Gulhi Falhu will increase its landmass by 50 hectares, while Hulhumalé has grown by 188 hectares since 1997, manifesting the city's ambition to keep up with its growth.

Velana International Airport, hovering centimeters above sea level, is just the first encounter a visitor makes with Malé's susceptibility to the ocean. The city's surrounding water is a constraint to sprawl, a danger to low-lying people and infrastructure, but also an opportunity to improve energy access and sustain housing needs.

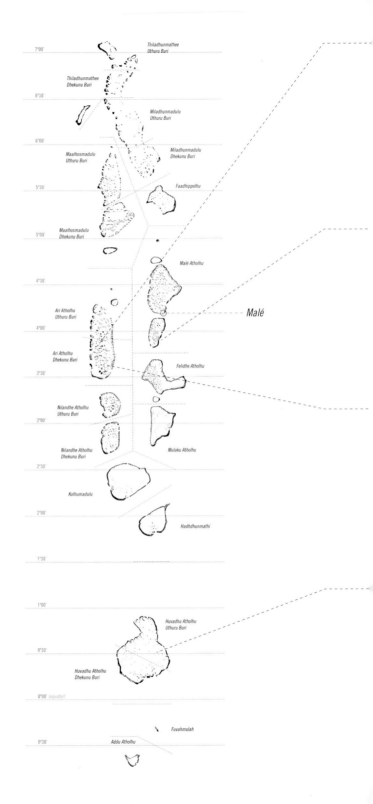

Thiladhunmathee Uthuru Buri

Thiladhunmathee Dhekunu Buri

Miladhunmadulu Uthuru Buri

Miladhunmadulu Dhekunu Buri

Maalhosmadulu Uthuru Buri

Faadhippolhu

Maalhosmadulu Dhekunu Buri

Malé Atholhu

Malé

Ari Atholhu Uthuru Buri

Ari Atholhu Dhekunu Buri

Felidhe Atholhu

Nilandhe Atholhu Uthuru Buri

Nilandhe Atholhu Dhekunu Buri

Mulaku Atholhu

Kolhumadulu

Hadhdhunmathi

Huvadhu Atholhu Uthuru Buri

Huvadhu Atholhu Dhekunu Buri

0°00' (equator)

Fuvahmulah

Addu Atholhu

Athuruga Resort, Ari Atholhu Dhekunu Buri

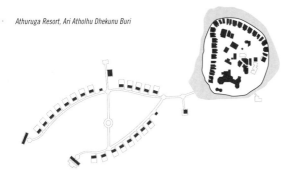

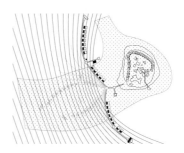

Cocoa Island Resort, Malé Atholhu

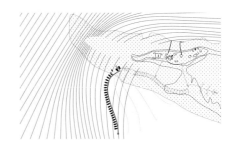

Centara Grand Island Resort and Spa, Ari Atholhu Dhekunu Buri

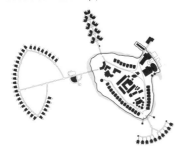

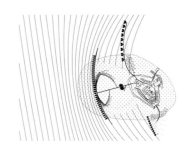

Park Hyatt Maldives Hadahaa, Huvadhu Atholhu Uthuru Buri

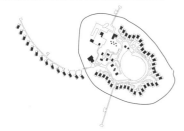

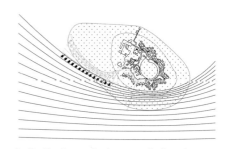

A sampling of resorts across the Maldives reveals unique patterns of organization oriented toward ideals of detachment and escape.

Considered from the perspective of energy generation, the resorts can be speculatively reorganized to follow each atoll's unique wave patterns, producing vastly different configurations.

The ongoing construction of a bridge linking Hulhumalé to Malé, and future plans to connect the city to Thilafushi, fundamentally alter Malé as an urban place. These new developments, far less dense than Malé proper, take on an antagonistic attitude toward water in a place irrevocably bound to it, promoting a paradigm of dryness.

With its highiest point reaching only 2.4 meters, Malé is directly threatened by sea-level rise and is hardly in a position to perpetuate regimes of low-lying land reclamation. Yet a more amphibious attitude is evident in the Maldives' many resort complexes, suggesting methods for reenvisioning Malé's development. Across the Maldives, novelty resorts have erected spaces that hover above the water, often built atop concrete piles, which allow visitors to inhabit the lagoon. The resorts take on a range of formations, from branch structures to rings, that rival the scale of the main island and offer a number of trajectories for considering waterborne planning.

Malé's bathymetry, typical of the country as a whole, fosters strong wave breaks due to the steep reef slope that surrounds it. While great for surfing, strong waves also overtop revetments and erode shores, challenging the casual nature of terrestrial life there. Yet the incessant barrage of waves also suggests an opportunity to exploit wave power for energy generation. On Malé, waves arrive from the south and break most strongly on the eastern shore where the reef plateaus. The Gaadhoo Koa, as this channel is known, is rich with potential for design exploration. While the city's surrounding water is a constraint to sprawl and a danger to people and infrastructure in low-lying areas, it is also an opportunity to improve energy access and sustain housing demand.

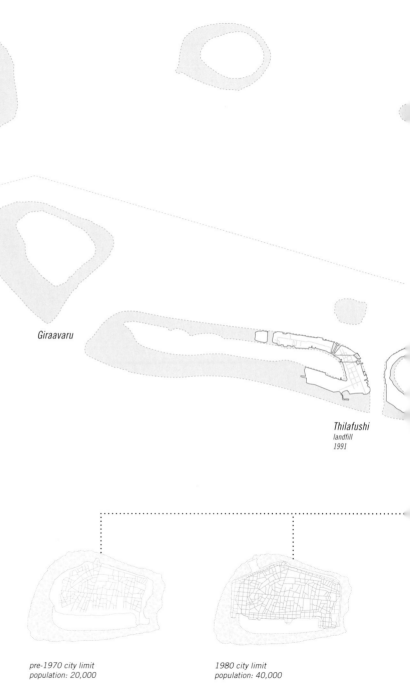

Giraavaru

Thilafushi
landfill
1991

[1] Republic of Maldives Ministry of Tourism, Statistics and Research Section, *Tourism Yearbook 2016* (Malé: Ministry of Tourism, 2016).

[2] National Bureau of Statistics, Maldives Population and Housing Census 2014 (Malé: National Bureau of Statistics, 2015), 33, http://statisticsmaldives.gov.mv/nbs/wp-content/uploads/2015/10/Census-Summary-Tables1.pdf.

[3] National Bureau of Statistics, 33.

[4] Ove Arup & Partners, "Feasibility Study for Construction of a Bridge between Malé and Hulhumalé: Final Report," August 2011, 3, www.environment.gov.mv/v1/download/312.

[5] Ove Arup & Partners, 7.

pre-1970 city limit
population: 20,000

1980 city limit
population: 40,000

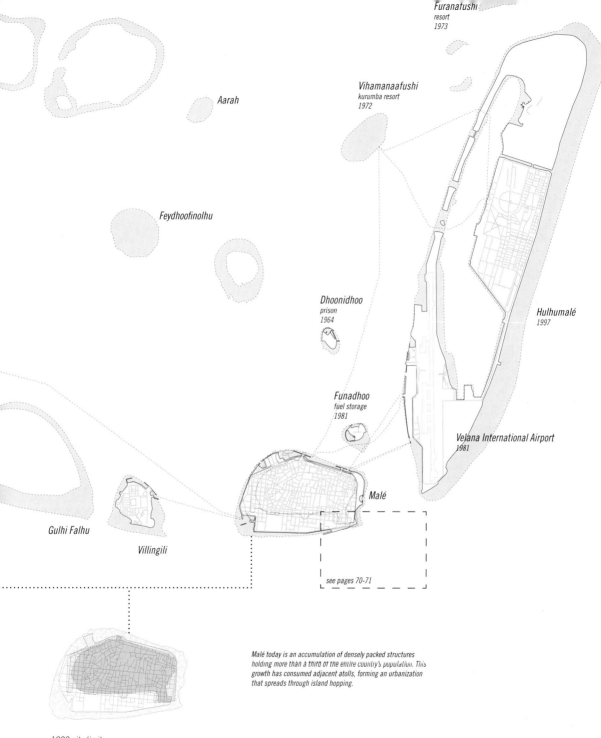

Furanafushi
resort
1973

Aarah

Vihamanaafushi
kurumba resort
1972

Feydhoofinolhu

Hulhumalé
1997

Dhoonidhoo
prison
1964

Funadhoo
fuel storage
1981

Velana International Airport
1981

Malé

Gulhi Falhu

Villingili

see pages 70-71

Malé today is an accumulation of densely packed structures
holding more than a third of the entire country's population. This
growth has consumed adjacent atolls, forming an urbanization
that spreads through island hopping.

1990 city limit
population: 55,130

41

Suspended Existence

Humankind's approach to establishing place is a complex of ordering, shaping, and making—resulting in seemingly homogenous desires of possession and ownership. Relative to our mammalian counterparts, humankind's disparate intentions of possession have culminated in a perverse human-centric approach to place: habitation and settlement in isolation from ecological systems. A contemporary example is Cadiz Inc.'s proposal to pump 814 billion gallons of water from under the unsettled Mojave Desert hundreds of miles west to the urban oases of Los Angeles and other Southern California communities. In contrast to this human-centric approach, human habitation patterns generated thousands of years ago survive in our ability to understand terrain through physical features and define place by distinct geographic characteristics.

Epochs passed, mammals evolved, and settlements grew in complexity, as establishment of "place" was linked to ideas of economic and cultural investment. Humans developed a false sense of ownership and presumed authority over terra firma and associated ecological networks. Geographic surveying of land gave humans the ability to define and navigate the world, developing a series of abstract borders that divide terrain into parcels for ownership and control, which served as a pretext for inhabiting and operating a site independently from its surrounding environmental contexts. The concept of the environment as an entity to be mapped, parceled, and owned specific to the interests of humankind uncovers a fundamental shift in thinking: settlement based on property in opposition to terrain.

Human settlement, or urbanism, is an aggregation of properties grounded in the static character of terra firma, constructed according to the patterns and flows of human economies. The relentless subdivision of environment has disrupted interconnected ecological networks and fostered a mode of superficial habitation—that is, inhabitation without habitat. The resulting urban fabric, often defined by abstract grid patterns, is composed of infrastructural systems constructed in accordance with monetary investments and ease of assembly rather than environmental character and ecological networks.

When parceled environments are conceived in isolation from the ecologies they exist within, a rift between human-centric settlement agendas and consequence is reinforced. Parceled urbanism overrides ecological networks with political, social, and economic agendas, thereby threatening its own sustained existence. While the frameworks responsible for urbanism's formal configurations are slow to change, today the surrounding environmental configurations are evolving at a rapid rate. Static principles of boundary, parcel, and property work in opposition to environments in constant flux, thus calling into question humankind's ability to frame the ecological agenda of our constructed habitats.

New Orleans manifests the abstracted parceling of land for purposes of distribution. The resulting grid, disassociated from fluctuating natural forces, is perceived as permanent and stable, yet it is often disrupted when natural geological features expand and contract.

The informal settlements pictured above share a similar scale and approach to habitat as the formal settlements of New Orleans; however, the shifts in geometry and variation in pattern reflect an idea of flexible (and, at times, adaptive) habitation. The absence of a grid determining flows, movements, and parcels allows for an urbanism more closely linked to natural geographies.

Ubiquity of Urban Sprawl

The ubiquity of urban sprawl reinforces a conscious segregation between human settlement and land, resulting in a "site-less" condition. The urban strategy identified here denies the specificity of site, instead following construction and material logics that generate a man-made environment of sameness. The resultant is the active disengagement of human settlement from surrounding environmental conditions. Dividing the environment into salable parcels results in a disrupted ecological network spanning across the territory. Moments of isolation and convenience mask uncertainty and questions of permanence.

Chauvin, Louisiana (partial map)

A rural territory between the Atchafalaya and Mississippi deltas, Chauvin represents a concentration of inhabitation around water systems—both man-made and natural. Instances of the settlement appear as discretized remnants of "site-less" developments imported from foreign contexts, while other parts illustrate an intimate response to the relationship of terra firma/aqua firma and its environmental setting. The left portion of the map shows how terrain is shaped by property lines and water-channel-control mechanisms.

Dulac, Louisiana (partial map)

A rural community existing around the fingers of Bayou Teche, Dulac is shaped by both the terra-firma edge condition and the movement of goods. But changing edge conditions and fluctuating intensities in water level have necessitated adaptations to the site. Similar to Chauvin, Dulac exists as a hybrid of site-less repetitive development mixed with site-specific floating and stilted structures. How does increased flexibility and adaptation provide clarity to an emergent typology?

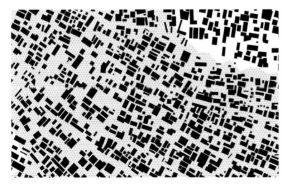

Makoko, Lagos, Nigeria (partial map)

Lagos responds to evolving edge conditions, offering alternative ways of building and organizing that are unfamiliar to a contemporary Western understanding of urban fabric and material and tectonic pursuits. The West African settlement, situated between two distinct environments—water and land—exposes the necessity to adapt to a shifting set of conditions. Wood-stilted settlements were constructed within the transitional zone between the grounded architecture of terra firma and floating structures of aqua firma. The architecture of Lagos is constantly adapting to the surface condition, calling into question the very definition of ground. The settlement's engagement with aqua firma reflects the movement of dugout canoes and fluctuating tides. Rather than being divided up as property, Lagos negotiates inhabitation in response to the site's fluctuations.

low stilted   high stilted   open stilted

commercial

infrastructure

service

residential

44

extrusion   *aggregated*

Cocodrie Stilted Architecture

Driving through southern Louisiana, one will find the region's entanglement with water on display. Residential structures, fire stations, industrial facilities, community structures, and institutions all delaminate from the ground plane, emphasizing through built form the fluctuating characteristic of water's surface. Stilted architecture is a dominant typology here, forming an ingrained culture of building. This photographic taxonomy represents the various methods of "stilting," as well as modes of integration, disguise, and functionalism. These systems propose a range of programmatic functions—individual, communal, temporary, and permanent—for both consistent and sporadic occupant use.

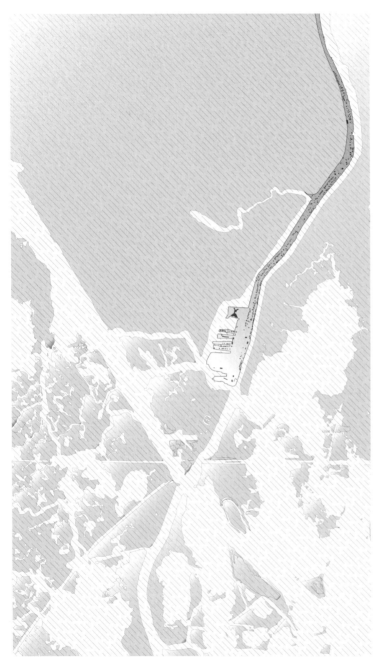

Lower Louisiana is in a constant state of change; delineating solid ground is a relentless and seemingly impossible task as the site shifts between terra firma and aqua firma. Fresh water from the Mississippi and Atchafalaya Rivers flowing from the north meets the salty water of the Gulf of Mexico, and lush native flora, offering agricultural potential, is complemented by plentiful land and water fauna.

The delta's fertile ground and ubiquitous water bodies have lured humankind to the murky region for centuries. As settlers' wealth grew, so too did the population of the delta, driving the construction of settlements around sites of resource extraction and channels for the multi-modal transportation of goods, people, and resources. Resource extraction and marine transport continue to accrue wealth to "big" industry, promoting ongoing occupation and settlement of the region. The inhabitation of the delta evolved similarly to other urban settlements, as systems of ownership drove the parceling of land into abstractly bounded sites. This pattern of generating static property ignores existing ecological networks and the delta's dynamic nature. It is within these shifting waters and the human-centric settlements of the delta that the superficiality of safe inhabitance and permanence develops.

> *These higher levees would almost certainly subject the other side of the river with its lower banks and sizable tributaries to catastrophic flooding, but one Delta planter estimated in 1858 that a good flood control system could bring local property values in the basin up to an aggregate total of approximately $150 million over the next decade.*
> *— James C. Cobb,* The Most Southern Place on Earth, *1992*

Left, *The Cocodrie region site plan illustrates the discretized zones of terra firma in juxtaposition to man-made and natural forces and waterways.*

Below, *A series of simple solid/void diagrams illustrates the relationship of program to ground. The leftmost configurations display a direct relationship; serial flooding has led to the development of elevated programs. Simple typologies include grounded program, raised program, and a hybrid raised/grounded program where the lower program is often sacrificed in periods of high water.*

Cocodrie, Louisiana, located in Terrebonne Parish, lies at the confluence of forces embedded within the delta and is facing the impact of rising water levels, erosion, and increased storm severity and frequency. Along the slender fingerlike stretches of terra firma, Cocodrie precariously congeals into a community, hosting roads, above- and belowground utilities, public spaces, private developments, and varying scales and densities of inhabitation. Incessant storm surges and rising sea levels are facts of life, requiring an understanding of and response to aquatic living conditions. The Federal Emergency Management Agency must work to adapt American urbanism to the aquatic conditions of the delta region—its current policy framework has been constructed by habitual recognition of the coming and going of water through stilted architecture. It must learn to understand the landscape as equally defined by aqua firma and terra firma.

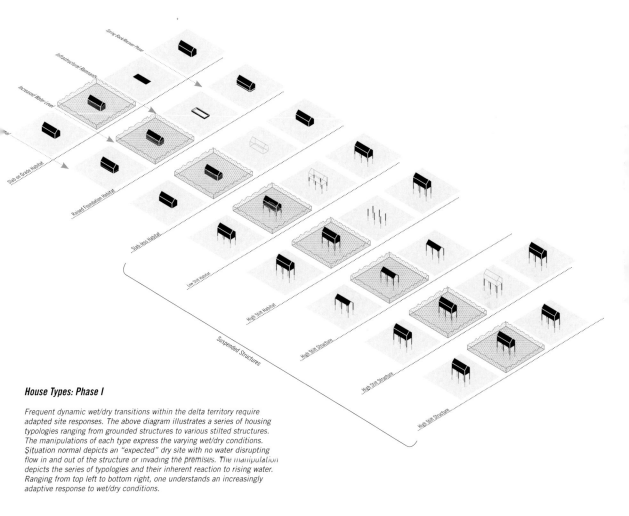

House Types: Phase I

Frequent dynamic wet/dry transitions within the delta territory require adapted site responses. The above diagram illustrates a series of housing typologies ranging from grounded structures to various stilted structures. The manipulations of each type express the varying wet/dry conditions. Situation normal depicts an "expected" dry site with no water disrupting flow in and out of the structure or invading the premises. The manipulation depicts the series of typologies and their inherent reaction to rising water. Ranging from top left to bottom right, one understands an increasingly adaptive response to wet/dry conditions.

broken world thinking

Kiel Moe

Montparnasse derailment, 1895.

[1] Merritt Roe Smith and Leo Marx, eds., *Does Technology Drive History? The Dilemma of Technological Determinism* (Cambridge, MA: MIT Press, 1994).

[2] "When you invent the ship, you also invent the shipwreck; when you invent the plane, you also invent the plane crash; and when you invent electricity, you invent electrocution. . . . Every technology carries its own negativity, which is invented at the same time as technical progress." Paul Virilio, *Politics of the Very Worst* (New York: Semiotext(e), 1999), 89.

[3] Ulrich Beck, *World at Risk* (London: Polity Press, 2009).

[4] Steven J. Jackson, "Rethinking Repair," in *Media Technologies: Essays on Communication, Materiality and Society*, ed. Tarleton Gillespie, Pablo Boczkowski, and Kirsten Foot (Cambridge, MA: MIT Press, 2014), 222.

[5] Jackson, 222.

[6] David Harvey, "The Fetish of Technology: Causes and Consequences," *Macalester International* 13 (2003): 3–30.

Relentless technological determinism was, and remains, a central impetus of modernity.[1] This routinely reductive determinism was characterized by a twofold belief: that problems had solutions and that new materials and technologies were primary indicators and enablers of progress. This aberrant form of rationality persists today and haunts some of our most troubling collective conditions, such as resource consumption, growing economic inequality, and climate change. In our current and future context, progress will have an entirely different character than what modernist ideologies trained us to believe.

While often couched in platitudes about innovation and progress, the reality today is that purportedly new materials, techniques, and technologies are more often engaged for the purposes of short-term market differentiation in neoliberal academic and professional contexts. This habit is perpetuated with little attention to the broader effects of the "new" technology or technique's consequences. Protagonists seem only concerned with capabilities of techne, never its culpabilities. As such, today there is nothing more conventional than incessant claims about innovation.

Rather than perpetuating these ideologies of progress as correlated with material and technological solutions to reductive problems, today's design culture needs a more frank, optimistic, and enabling account of both technology and progress. One of the central limitations of modernity's technological determinism was that it would never admit to or anticipate its own failures. To paraphrase the philosopher Paul Virilio, to invent the ship is, simultaneously, to also invent the shipwreck.[2] In the name of progress, modernity ignored this simultaneous failure of technology, triggering a stark asymmetry between technology's capabilities and its culpabilities. A "solution" was thus typically connected to the immediate "problem" and systemically made to occlude its own risks and failures. That is to say, a solution tended to ignore the constitutive complexity of the systems in which it was enmeshed: the history, politics, culture, and ecology that precondition the application of any technology, and that follow it.

In modernity, a failure might be associated directly with technological objects—like the ship and the shipwreck—but given modernity's metabolic and political rifts, the failure of a technology also occurred in more far-flung contexts. Think about the example of a car. There is the invention of the car and the car crash, but there is also the slower and more extended crash of ecological systems that are inextricable from its production, operation, and associated infrastructure. In other words, one of the prime failures of modernism's technological determinism is its paradoxical foundation: we granted technology agency to change life in the name of progress while simultaneously and opportunistically granting it autonomy by externalizing its systemic consequences for life. In this incongruous positivistic faith, technology could only do good, and should a vexing problem or consequence arise in the use of the technology, then more technology was certainly the solution.

This is the fiction that has repeatedly enabled technological determinist ideologies of progress. But it is increasingly difficult to maintain the conceits and externalities associated with this version of progress. We can no longer so easily uncouple "bads" from "goods." The negative effects of the car—climate-changing pollution or car-centric city planning, for example—are perhaps slightly more apparent today, even if the full consequences of the automobile are scarcely imaginable in our modernist minds. The problem-solution mentality of the narrowly construed technological object merely postpones the inevitable crash or failure of the object in its larger system, usually for a generation or two. This mentality makes the future a colony of present technological determinism.

A different ontology of progress is necessary for this century. Designers, in particular, need to learn to situate the goods and bads of a technology or technique within a much larger system boundary of lived life, given the precarious ecological, social, and political contexts that condition design today. So in a gush of goodwill in light of what Ulrich Beck describes as our collective "risk society,"[3] it is refreshing and worthwhile to reason and imagine failure, entropy, and inextricable effects as inherent to an evolved conception of progress.

This involves what the computer scientist Steven J. Jackson calls "broken world thinking." As an alternative to our habitual way of thinking about technology, Jackson asks, "What happens when we take erosion, breakdown, and decay, rather than novelty, growth, and progress, as our starting points in thinking?"[4] He goes on: "Broken world thinking is both normative and ontological, in the sense that it makes claims about the nature of technology and its relationship to broader social worlds, some of which may differ from deep-rooted cultural assumptions. But it is also empirical and methodological, an argument and provocation toward doing new and different kinds of research, and new and different kinds of politics, in media and technology studies today."[5]

In other words, designers would do well to cultivate optimism and intelligence about the inevitable outcomes—and failures—of our technological society and in turn develop an appreciation for the enabling social and practical systems that emerge in the aftermath once things break down. This is an entirely different characterization of progress: one that is more emancipatory in its politics and convivial in its techniques, and less hubristic in its promises.

The aim is to not to learn to "fix" what is broken in a technological object or system.[6] As David Harvey demonstrates, a technological fix has more to do with the entrenchment of systems, knowledge, and practices, much like how he describes "spatial fixes" in geography. In other words, fixing only ossifies the broken system— the exact opposite of meaningful progress. Nor is the aim to learn tricks and develop designs for how life can persist as it is now, as in the "sustainability" discourse, or for how life can snap easily back to where it was, as in the "resilience" discourse. Rather than persisting or returning to the same comfortable state, progress by definition is suggestive of the next state, an evolutionary unfolding of both object and environment.

In this regard, broken world thinking offers a way to conceive how systems reconfigure, reassemble, and reconstitute toward their next state. This type of thinking can develop an ethics of care and repair as a constitutive attribute of life with technological systems in this century. The design of maintenance, next uses, and repurposing suggests an entirely different conception of material and social progress. This is an overt challenge to the tyranny of the early modernist, and now neoliberal, ideology of "innovation" and growth as indicators of progress.

Broken world thinking also challenges the false modernist binary of technological escalation as one dominant ideology and Luddism as its minor other. Both are recidivist positions, and this binary is chauvinistic and regressive. A more optimistic, productive, and astute—if not nonmodern—paradigm focuses more squarely on actual technological outcomes and efficacy rather than ever-escalating promises. The breakdown of a technological system reveals more about progress than any blustery marketing of "innovation." Indeed, the consequences of systemic ecological, social, and political disruptions and disrepair associated with a new technology or technique far outpace the short-term market differentiations associated with "disruption" in contemporary marketing jargon. Broken world thinking helps reframe progress.

In this century progress must itself be redesigned. Actual social, political, ecological, and architectural advancements will not arise from exhausted treadmills of technological escalation or from neoliberal innovation or disruption jargon. Emancipation from the fetters of this persistent technological determinism is essential to the design of progress. More convivial—and less proprietary—technological systems that aid, rather than limit, collective evolution toward next states are also essential.

On the crumbling edge of modernity's physical and intellectual infrastructure, it is indeed progressive to think through how seemingly steady-state worlds break down and then reassemble. The evolution of our society, our politics, and our ecology in this century will be intimately connected to a non-steady-state conception of our worlds. Thus, how an ethics of care and repair unfolds beyond the modernist ideologies of progress—such as in the shipbreaking practices on the coasts of Bangladesh or in the repair and repurposing of cell phones in India or Africa—is instructive for how we might more progressively envision nonhuman infrastructure, town-breaking designs, or the architecture of large populations migrating to new contexts. The redesign of progress—guided by what it convivially enables, how it emancipates, and how it helps us evolve—is a salient question for architecture today. This demands new objects and subjects of design, and warrants a fresh look at what design can do, and how it will fail, as a means forward in this century's non-steady-state contexts.

Kiel Moe is an architect and an associate professor at Harvard University Graduate School of Design.

III. LEAVING

The acceptance of and commitment to resettlement does not guarantee that it will occur at the pace the rising sea will demand. For those communities likely to be uprooted, short- and long-term relocation can be a means to navigate logistical and political hardships. The mobility of a floating settlement provides independence for communities to escape the impact of natural disasters while finding economic prosperity in the oceans and seas.

Existing infrastructures such as seafaring vessels and buoyage would become the architectural tools for settling the oceans. Terrestrial and stationary concerns like differential structural settlement, floodplain exposure, and lateral stability are supplanted by issues of draft, listing, and metal fatigue. Basic needs, however, stay the same. Architecture's ability to provide shelter is multiplicitous and understood, but its capacity to assist in the acquisition of food and fresh water, and its affordances for identity, social participation, curiosity, and recreation are more complex.

When we refer to "bodies of water," we mean to suggest a humanization or personalization of the subject. Bodies are things central to a complex system, vessels containing vital and valuable material. We identify waters in this way because it allows us to reconcile their scale and power and to appreciate their virtuosity in a more sensitive way. We take care of bodies because a failure to do so has negative effects on the systems and apparatuses they support.

What is our responsibility to a body?

Global Hydrological System

When dry ground is represented as void, one can clearly depict the continuity of the wet. As water forms vary in scale and ecologies, the guiding principle to be understood is interconnectivity. The influence of one relatively small culture living adjacent to a freshwater stream can have global impacts on the hydrological system.

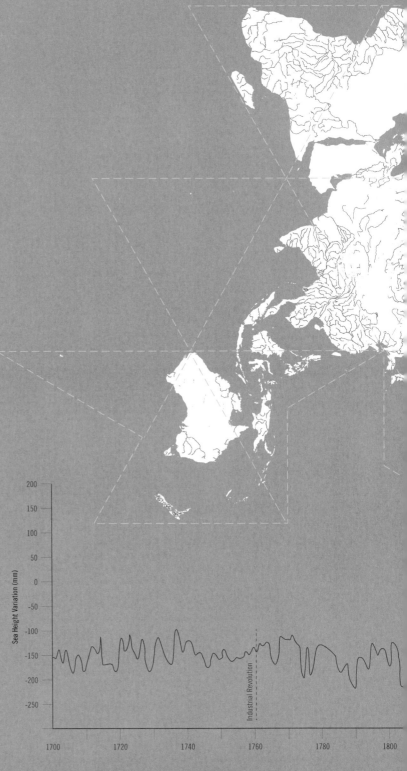

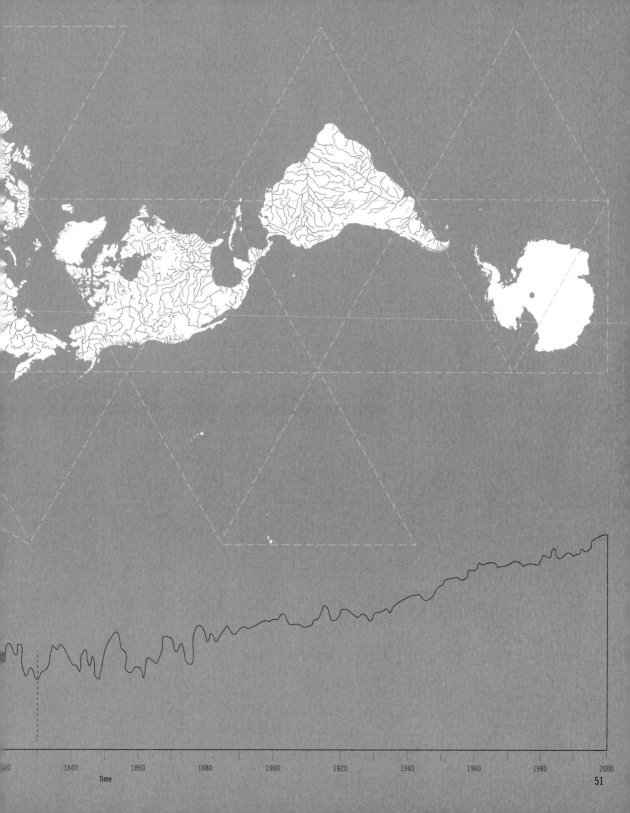

20   1840   1860   1880   1900   1920   1940   1960   1980   2000

Time

Shipbreakers, Fleet

The intimate knowledge of seafaring vessels accumulated through the practice of shipbreaking provides insight into the structural forms appropriate for a seaborne habitat. As water rises, construction begins in earnest atop the cargo hatches, reversing the typical model of dismantlement in favor of the deliberate planning and pursuit of new territory. The scale of bulk carriers and vessels like them affords a layering of residential uses with associated support programs like power production, desalination, sanitation, and communal spaces, all at sea. The vessels offer a short-term solution to the displacement of those living in impoverished communities, as well as longer-term options, should sociopolitical forces interfere with resettlement. When the world's largest crude carrier, *Mont* (earlier named *Seawise Giant* and *Jahre Viking*), ultimately landed in a shipbreaking yard in Alang, India, its dismantling required eighteen thousand workers. Owing to both the scale of the work involved and the repetitive and haphazard dismantling process, shipbreaking culture already possesses notions of cooperation and participation that are associated with vibrant communities. These qualities, coupled with the absolute population and relative density offered by the ship, foster hope for the resettlement of these communities in more favorable conditions.

Dwelling blocks are fabricated on the horizontally sliding cargo-hold doors of the bulk carriers' decks. Upon departure, the doors (and therefore the dwellings) can be adjusted according to the course of the ship, optimizing for direct sunlight to all the units while managing the balance of the ship as a whole.

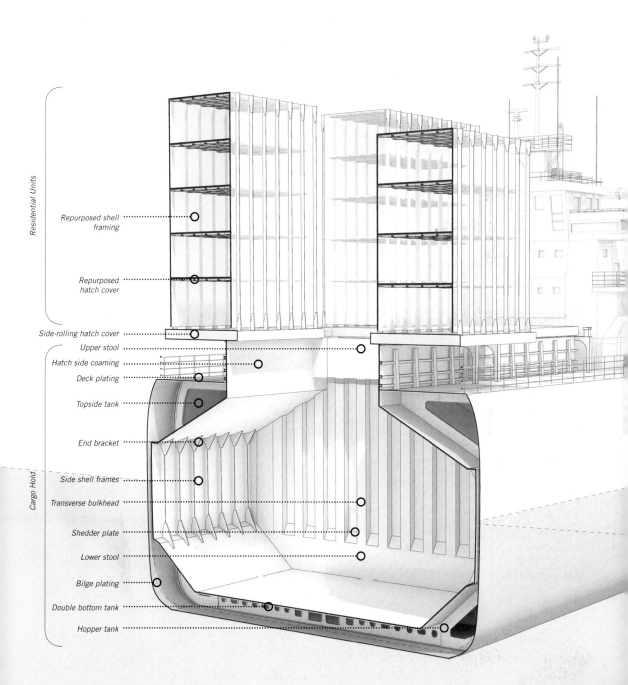

Residential Units

Repurposed shell framing

Repurposed hatch cover

Side-rolling hatch cover

Upper stool

Hatch side coaming

Deck plating

Topside tank

End bracket

Side shell frames

Transverse bulkhead

Shedder plate

Lower stool

Bilge plating

Double bottom tank

Hopper tank

Cargo Hold

53

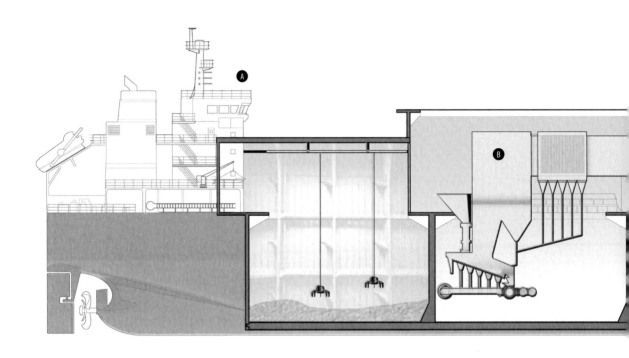

A

The ship's bridge retains its central functions but is retrofitted to control the ship's various processes and the vessel's role within the larger fleet. The bridge can also serve as a gathering place and a market for distributing goods and information or offer recreation and leisure as a display surface for projecting films.

B

The ready-made ships (and aggregated fleet) command a network of surface filtration buoys, acting as a collection point to gather detritus captured by the buoys. A waste-to-energy plant installed in sequential holds generates power and processes accumulated waste, aiding in the cleaning of its surrounding aquatic environment. Excess heat from energy generation is used to heat ballast water taken into the ship's hull. While ballast water discharge has been responsible for the introduction of invasive species and the global spread of diseases, heating the water with high-temperature air helps sterilize it.[1]

The fleet perpetuates the global practice of recycling steel. However, instead of distributing scrap to be cut and melted down, the new fleet reconstitutes its by-products for mobile living. These seafaring communities foster economies that are supplemented through extraction of waste from the global water systems and transportation of waste to collection sites for reallocation of value.

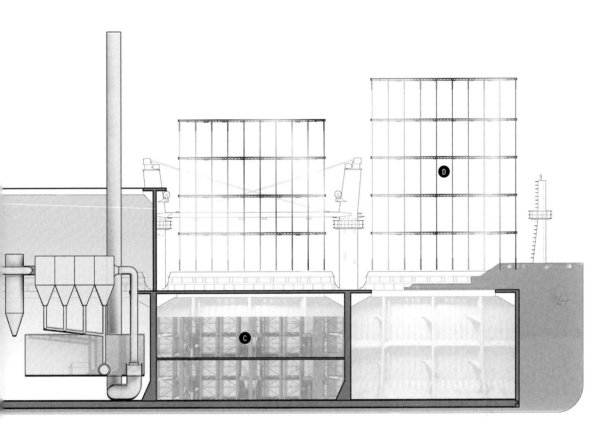

C

"Pinkhouses" constructed in the hold of the ship provide food and valuable nutrition to the ship's inhabitants.[2] The modest heat generated from the pinkhouses warms swimming pools throughout the ship.

D

Residential structures are built on top of the deck of the ship, taking on a variety of configurations based on the various programs nested in the ship's holds. Recreational pools and baths are filled with sanitized, desalinated, and filtered ballast water, providing needed outlets for stress relief in the small community.

[1] On the problems associated with ballast-water discharge, see Eugene H. Buck, "Ballast Water Management to Combat Invasive Species," *US Congressional Research Service Report No. RL32344*, April 10, 2012, https://fas.org/sgp/crs/misc /RL32344.pdf.

[2] On pinkhouses, see Michaeleen Deoucleff, "Vertical 'Pinkhouses': The Future of Urban Farming?," NPR, May 21, 2013, http://www.npr.org/sections /thesalt/2013/05/21/185758529/vertical-pinkhouses-the -future-of-urban-farming.

The grouping of multiple vessels into a fleet allows for the aggregation of larger settlements, which can be reconfigured, shuffled, and expanded as needed. The variety of vessel sizes and types has the potential to accommodate communities from a few hundred to as many as a few thousand people and support a diverse range of programs. Yet the proposed program shift, from material reuse to resource reallocation and community building, asks the question: do current methods of shipbreaking represent progress through the dismantling and recycling of refined materials, or are they simply human-centric economic frameworks?

Guiding Lights

Mobility is fundamental to an architecture of departure. As natural disasters occur with increasing frequency and severity, the fixed nature of cities becomes their greatest vulnerability. One need not look far into the past to find examples of urbanity crippled by natural disasters: Hurricane Katrina's impact on the Gulf of Mexico and New Orleans, Hurricane Sandy's effect on the Tri-State Area, and the devastation wreaked by the Tōhoku earthquake and tsunami on Japan are just a few cases in which fixity had serious consequences. If a vessel, a community, or even a metropolis were afforded the possibility of mobility, perhaps approaching dangers could be avoided or managed. How will a seaborne civilization know where impending danger will approach from and at what severity it will strike? If the knowledge pertaining to impending danger is available to a mobile city, how will the city know where to reposition itself to be out of harm's way and in safe waters?

The buoy has undergone major changes over its history, from small wooden cask to smart object to data-collection instrument twelve meters in diameter, morphing its shape and increasing in size and sophistication. Buoys today collect and transmit data related to subsurface characteristics and atmospheric properties. The existing infrastructures of buoys and markers already in use could be the foundation for creating a smart oceanic infrastructure. This network of buoys could be deployed to communicate information on the development of potential storms and natural events, guiding those in the path of destruction to safe waters.

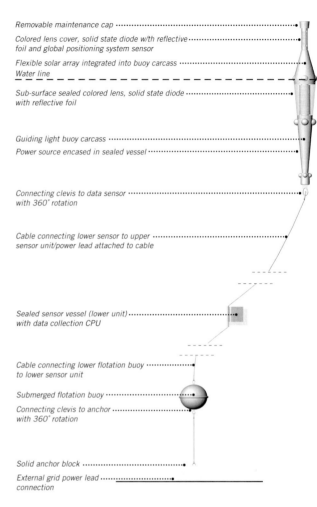

Removable maintenance cap

Colored lens cover, solid state diode w/th reflective foil and global positioning system sensor

Flexible solar array integrated into buoy carcass

Water line

Sub-surface sealed colored lens, solid state diode with reflective foil

Guiding light buoy carcass

Power source encased in sealed vessel

Connecting clevis to data sensor with 360° rotation

Cable connecting lower sensor to upper sensor unit/power lead attached to cable

Sealed sensor vessel (lower unit) with data collection CPU

Cable connecting lower flotation buoy to lower sensor unit

Submerged flotation buoy

Connecting clevis to anchor with 360° rotation

Solid anchor block

External grid power lead connection

Active amphibious zones in constant fluctuation depend on flexible infrastructures to communicate safe passage. The buoy provides a vertically mobile messaging system, communicating with vessels to help navigate shallow shipping lanes, or sending ahead warning of impending danger.

Surface Filtration Buoyage

A logical extension of the pollution identification buoy is the deployment of surface filtration buoys tasked with collecting on- and near-surface refuse. The filtration buoys extend the reach of the floating purification centers, increasing the overall collection area and yield.

Urbanization, overpopulation, and the push to and through the Industrial Revolution have taken their toll on the earth's ecologies, affecting both land and sea. The remnants of human excess have accumulated in the form of errant litter, landfills, illegal dumping in waters, and multiple floating mats of refuse in the oceans. The floating mats of refuse collect in the oceans' five gyres—located in the northern and southern Pacific, the northern and southern Atlantic, and in the Indian Ocean—and contain approximately 5.25 trillion pieces of plastic debris. This combination of intended and unintended debris settles in the oceans, either floating or suspended within its currents.

By targeting surface refuse, surface filtration buoys and ships can extract plastics before they have a chance to break down into microfibers, which would make the plastic pollution harder to filter out and cause more damage to the food chain. As the filtration buoys collect seaborne waste, they compact and shape it, blasting digital notifications when the buoy

reaches capacity. Vessels, similar to the Shipbreakers fleet, gather the packaged waste and stow it within the cargo holds of ships to be transported to land for sale. In tandem with identification buoyage and surface filtration buoyage, the ocean becomes an arable space, contributing to processes of energy generation while slowly undergoing its own rehabilitation.

An important aspect embedded within a floating, mobile city is its persistence, allowing it to continuously separate human-produced flotsam from the environment it is infiltrating. A network of buoys and pollution identification buoyage identify, quantify, and qualify the amount of particulate in the water, marking and monitoring areas of heavy pollution. By partitioning oceans, rivers, and lakes with notations from "heavily polluted" to "seemingly clean," the buoys can act as a means to identify where floating settlements should relocate and rehabilitate the water quality, offering the city as an agent: a floating purification center.

The refuse would become a valuable resource to the community, which could collect, pelletize, or bale it, and then sell it to countries as fuel for waste-to-energy or biomethanation processes.

Human refuse carelessly discarded accumulates around the globe; often dispersed through inland waterways and settling in the planet's seas. Vast quantities of garbage amass, destroying eco-sysems at a multi-plicity of scales and preventing natural aquatic growth.

Wind turbine ··············

Upper drive unit bearing/seal ··············
Attachment clevis (for offloading) ··············
Gear box/lower drive unit bearing/seal ··············
Aluminum hopper cage (removable) ··············
Discharge port ··············

Auger drive shaft ··············
Steel exo-skeleton at hopper ··············

Large volume hopper ··············
Uploading caisson ··············

Aluminum drainage grill ··············
Fibrous filter ··············
Upload debris auger ··············
Vertical steel exo-skeleton ··············
Slotted steel rotational collector ··············

Flotation vessel ··············
Download drive auger ··············
Downloading cylinder wall ··············

Discharge port ··············
Maintenance access port ··············
Upper drive unit bearing/seal gear box/lower drive unit bearing ··············

Structural fin ··············

Ballast tank ··············

Anchor clevis to drift sock ··············

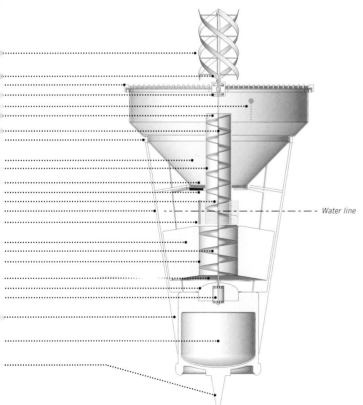

— Water line

IV. STAYING

The communities occupying soon-to-be submerged territories of low-lying coastal regions will lose more than just shelter. The loss of physical land, thought of as home or one's place of being, can also erase one's heritage. Much to the dismay of many, living and dying in certain coastal zones will cease to be an option. A shift in mind-set toward buoyancy for those committed to remaining in place offers the opportunity to evolve their culture while retaining their heritage. The essence of their culture will have the opportunity to be projected not only onto the surface of the rising sea but also into the future, as a new cultural chapter is written, one the sea cannot claim.

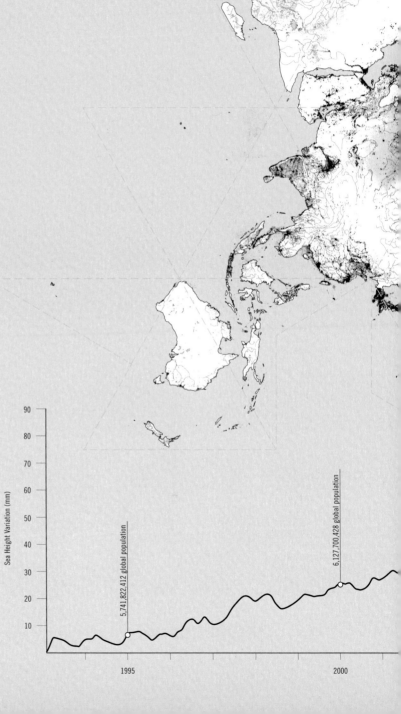

Finding Certain Ground

The opacity within the map represents the accumulation of human settlement, which is precariously often concentrated within littoral zones. As global population increases, the finite resource of dry ground causes an increase in settlement densities. Concurrently, rising sea levels are claiming new ground within these territories and forcing the question of where future expansion will occur. As new settlements continue to build up and down, expanding their z-axes in place, maximum densities will eventually be reached. How does the inevitable expansion of settlement foster dry and wet zones, and eventually create wet urban and city-scale settlements?

Sea Height Variation (mm)

90

80

70

60

50

40

30

20

10

5,741,822,412 global population

6,127,700,428 global population

1995

2000

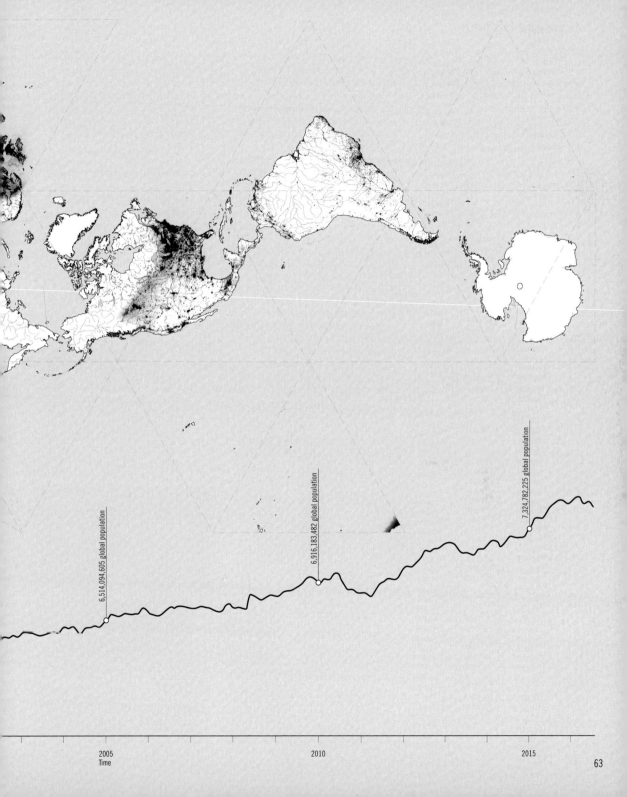

6,514,094,605 global population

6,916,183,482 global population

7,324,782,225 global population

2005
Time

2010

2015

63

Suspended Existence

The reconfiguration of terra firma across lower Louisiana negotiates pressure from environmental forces and man-made flood-control mechanisms, producing a deltascape of levees, cuts, and spillways. Two opposing forces are inflicting significant ecological change: rising sea levels push saltwater farther inland, destroying flora and exposing soil to increased erosion, while the constriction of the Atchafalaya and Mississippi Rivers by levees and control mechanisms also affects the distribution of silt across the delta, negatively dispersing terra firma and fostering an increasingly aquatic environment. Communities along the Gulf Coast are reconciling significant changes in the immediate future. Cocodrie, Louisiana, for example, will be an environment where terra firma will only exist below the water's surface, drowning the notion of a parceled environment. Settlement will continue in a very different environmental milieu, foreign to the principles from which it sprang. The stilted architecture of Cocodrie, hovering precariously above the water, will appear out of place in its own context; future development will comb the aquascape of the delta in search of landscape.

The dissolution of the static parcel boundary requires traditional urban strategies to be rethought. As water levels rise and terra firma erodes, the plausibility of ownership and property demarcation is washed away. A habitat and territory retaining a familiarity with industry, culture, and heritage has the potential to persist, but the methods of inhabitation must shift in response to changing environmental pressures and patterns. Place remains; boundary and parcel dissolve. Linear edges and conceptual borders based on property and ownership are substituted with anchor points, respecting bathymetry and the force of water.

The use of anchor points supplants the existing frameworks of static foundations, parceling, and property specific to human inhabitation, and distinguishes a divergent, fluid trajectory of settlement. The recognition of residence as an ecological approach positions the intention of human settlement and environment in balance and displaces human-centric agendas. A flexible connection between settlement and terra firma establishes two distinct principles: the overlay and the reconfiguration. The overlay allows for the possibility of occupiable overlapping zones, not dedicating a specific parcel or area of land to an individual, bounded site. In addition, decoupling settlement from ground allows for the reconfiguration of community as environmental pressures ebb and flow. Reconfiguration in littoral zones proceeds with respect to bathymetric change,

tidal-flow patterns, hydrological forces, and shifting ecological networks to attain sustained existence. New communities that are developed in accordance with these principles displace the human-centric approach to urbanism to enable an ecologically based dialogue between site, settlement, and inhabitant.

The redefinition of territory from a division between terra firma and aqua firma to a dynamic aqua firma repositions questions of resource extraction, distribution, and allocation. How does this, in turn, foster a shift in the perception of resource allocation, in terms of stability and durability? How does a renewed connection to site conditions and ecologies shift the inhabitant's expectations for a city constructed within littoral zones? Can this projective urbanism provide dynamic living bounds versus static living sites that accommodate flexible habits and patterns? This shift in perception will be a necessity for sustained human settlement within littoral zones.

The apparent ease with which fortunes were made in the delta seemed to make some planters almost oblivious not just to debt but to the ease with which their riches could be lost.
—James C. Cobb, The Most Southern Place on Earth, *1992*

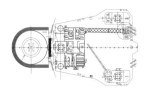

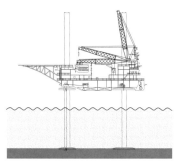

Sailboats moored off Catalina Island, a coastal community in Southern California. The moored vessels align themselves in a natural arc, responding to the contextual parameters of water and land. A single anchor point, or mooring, determines the space between vessels that allows them to shift and reorient with the flow and movement of the water.

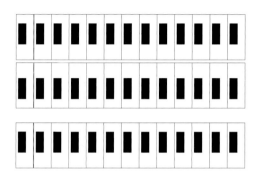

Static and parceled developments are configured as synonymous, repetitive blocks. While a group of parcels aggregate into a block or neighborhood, the parcels function individually and allow for private boundaries, exterior spaces, interior spaces, and circulation. The layout does not allow for the planned developments to overlap or adjust to the fluid and dynamic environment.

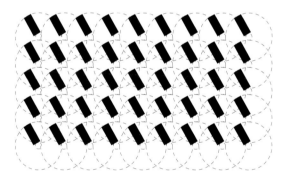

The deletion of parcels with static boundaries allows new strategies of settlement movement in a dynamic environment. The introduction of mooring and tethering defines new spatial parameters centered on a single anchor point. This flexible connection can accommodate planned currents and fluid shifts.

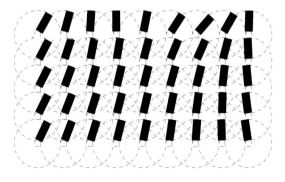

Unplanned shifts and movements caused by storm surges, water fluctuations, and evolving water patterns can also be accommodated by the individual settlements through anchoring strategies. Settlements move freely—some may remain in their current position while others respond to an imposing force.

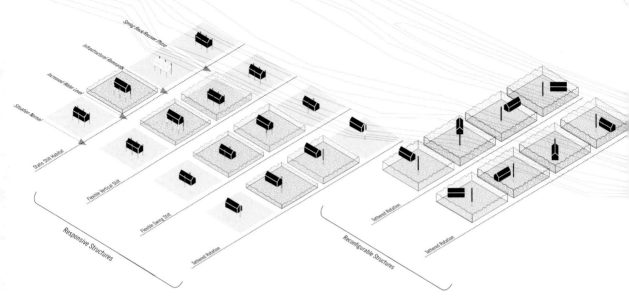

House Types: Phase II

Frequent dynamic transitions between wet and dry within the Delta territory require current housing typologies to adapt. The above diagram illustrates a series of housing typologies ranging from grounded structures to various stilted structures. The manipulations of each type express the varying wet/dry conditions. Situation normal depicts an "expected" dry site with water neither disrupting the flow in and out of the structure nor invading the premises. The manipulation depicts the series of evolving stilted typologies and their inherent reaction to rising water. Viewing the diagram from top left to bottom right, one understands an increasingly adaptive response to wet/dry conditions.

Phase II introduces the concept of mooring that allows the reconfiguration of settlement layout through a tethered rotation pattern.

Tethered Settlement

The proposed site is a reconfigured extension from existing settlement patterns previously established in terra firma. Suspended mooring provides flexibility in place as movement within a larger system. A single settlement or aggregate of settlements can migrate within the fluid environment through a temporary release of the tethering agent, fostering a positive shift between buoyant and anchored strategies.

Projective settlements reinforce existing settlement strategies that are located as a response to economic and cultural habits of resource extraction. Resource sites, illustrated through the solid zones, define the settlement migrating patterns. The fluidity between the wet and the dry conditions within the same zone accommodates a shift in scale and program. Jack-up barges, using the same mooring strategies as residences, will host the industrial processing of resource extraction and distribution. They can then move onto the next site with the residences free to follow.

Inhabitable Wave Farm

Water is the city of Malé's most valuable resource. While historically used for the direct discharge of sewage and reclaimed on an as-needed basis, the sea that surrounds the city—which will one day consume much of it—has to be considered as an asset. Desalination and other processes abstract the value of water in the quotidian life of Malé; other than a site for surfing and fishing, water is seen as an impediment to the city's ambition.

Malé's eventual inundation will lead to changes to the use and character of the city, but its role as a hub for travel suggests that its abandonment is unlikely. Instead, the displaced ground-level occupancy of the city will be shifted vertically and horizontally, including to new floating spaces designed for dynamic and flexible occupancy.

Resort structures in the Maldives employ architectural novelty as a means of building cachet. While more hedonistic than utilitarian, the resorts' architectural approaches may be relevant to a projective envisioning of Malé in the future. The scale of resort architecture is such that it may not offer a meaningful housing strategy, and thatched roofs may be just an aesthetic appliqué. Yet the Maldives' waterborne structures and the resultant mesh skirts for lounging and water access offer not just a technique for addressing Malé's future programming needs but also a means for imbuing life there with the qualities and opportunities often reserved for deep-pocketed guests.

A network of energy generating point absorbers hosts an evolving collection of programs, including fishing stands, surf launches, and residences. A system of brackets and slides allows for structures to span the point absorbers as they rise, fall, and sway with the waves. Since they are accessed by boat or foot, blocks can be organized and oriented

Point absorbers sited deeper in the channel can provide fishermen with access to ocean life typically found farther from shore.

Enshrouding the point absorbers in a flexible high mil membrane allows multiple units to be linked and traversed, producing an inhabitable matrix that serves at once as promenade, dock, playground, and energy source.

to optimize energy generation in relation to a range of factors, from wave patterns to localized bathymetries, to good spots for fishing, surfing, or docking.

The submerged atoll—a seamount, in technical parlance—acts as an anchor to moor a dynamic floating settlement. The communities who have called the land home identify historically and culturally significant sites to guide the construction of the newly formed city. The new settlement in turn acts as a foundation for the communities to begin the construction of their future history. Projective housing prototypes capable of rising within their foundation piers respond to the scale and social structures of the particular site. Lift generated by wave power is converted to electrical energy through point absorbers over the piers. The vertical movement of the housing as it responds to the waves drives mechanical stroking to power an electric generator.

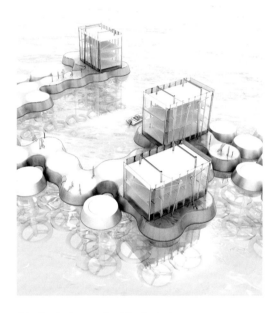

Using the absorbers as a foundation for structures, the membrane also supports residential and communal life through forms of connection calibrated to the island's daily routines.

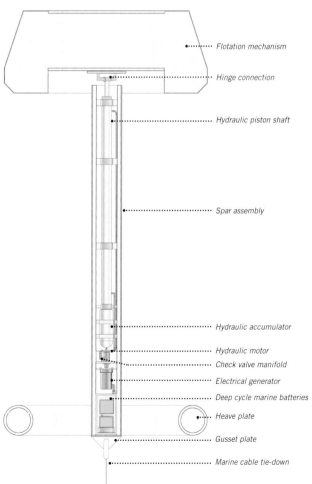

Flotation mechanism

Hinge connection

Hydraulic piston shaft

Spar assembly

Hydraulic accumulator

Hydraulic motor

Check valve manifold

Electrical generator

Deep cycle marine batteries

Heave plate

Gusset plate

Marine cable tie-down

73° 30' 54" E   73° 31' 0" E   73° 31' 6" E

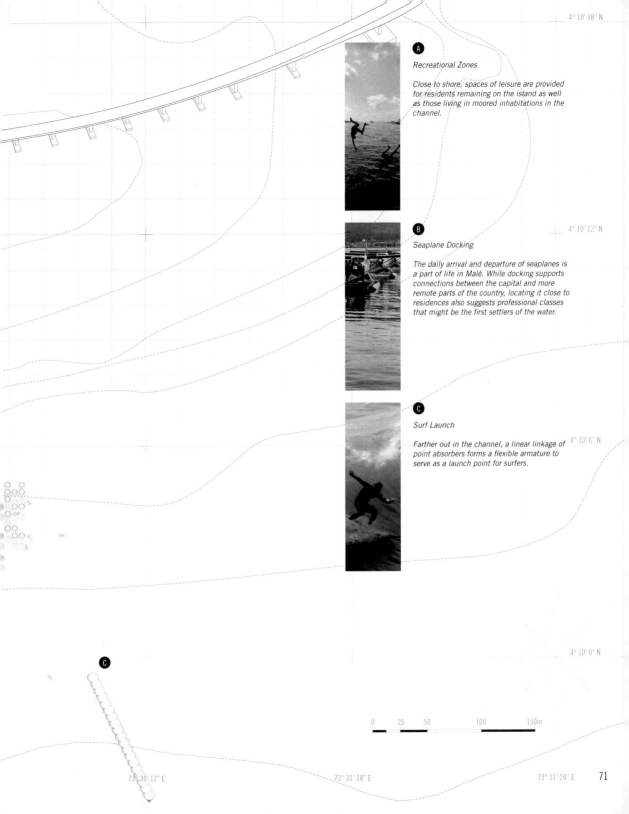

A

Recreational Zones

Close to shore, spaces of leisure are provided
for residents remaining on the island as well
as those living in moored inhabitations in the
channel.

B

Seaplane Docking

The daily arrival and departure of seaplanes is
a part of life in Malé. While docking supports
connections between the capital and more
remote parts of the country, locating it close to
residences also suggests professional classes
that might be the first settlers of the water.

C

Surf Launch

Farther out in the channel, a linear linkage of
point absorbers forms a flexible armature to
serve as a launch point for surfers.

C

| 0 | 25 | 50 | 100 | 150m |

Submerged Being

As the rising sea engulfs low-lying island nations, the once-inhabitable ground slowly submerges, out of sight, but remains rich with cultural memory. While the civilization that once walked its shores becomes placeless, the land itself becomes a new place, eroded and consumed by the water's relentless currents and invaded by new marine inhabitants. These forces conspire to corrupt the traces of the now-displaced people's relationship to the land, their ancestors, and their culture.

What value do humans provide in mapping and annotating the disappearing history and culture that the lost land carries? Seafaring culture relies on the clear description and demarcation of subsurface terrain to ensure the safe navigation of the water's surface and the avoidance of seamounts, guyots, and lagan. Buoyage has long been used as a means of marking subsurface conditions in efforts to communicate the safe passage of waterways, by telling the story unfolding just below the surface. As the sea immerses the land belonging to past civilizations, the opportunity to map the historical significance of these populations arises. Using the language of buoyage, the people who once belonged to the sunken land can communicate their past existence to the world, projecting it onto the surface of the water.

An environment in flux represents a liability in the eyes of humankind, which no amount of human effort can combat. Inhabitants of the Mississippi River and Atchafalaya River Deltas will soon face what no culture is prepared to absorb—the erosion and submersion of the terra firma that they are bound to. Southern Louisiana's slow retreat into the murky waters of the delta will separate the people from elements of their cultural identity that are embedded in that place and have been fostered over a prolonged existence on its surface. As the future of a community's existence negotiates looming termination, the question will change from how to exist to what will be lost. The rising water and the eroding terra firma have brought forth our declaration in regard to the importance of cultural identity; we must question our trajectory as a species and reframe the meaning of cultural identity.

East-West Sections through Isle de Jean Charles

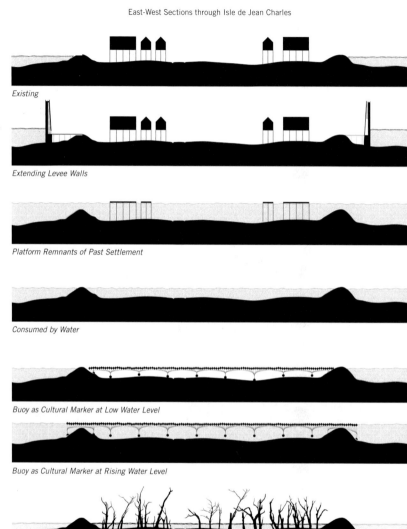

Existing

Extending Levee Walls

Platform Remnants of Past Settlement

Consumed by Water

Buoy as Cultural Marker at Low Water Level

Buoy as Cultural Marker at Rising Water Level

Oak Forest as Cultural Marker

The top section illustrates the existing relationship of Isle de Jean Charles with the surrounding body of water. Subsequently, a series of sections project future scenarios for the island—all but one suggest that human inhabitants have vacated the island, though the cultural heritage once present lingers on through a variety of cultural markers. The single scenario that projects human settlement to subsist requires the vertical extension and fortification of existing levee walls.

Satellite images show the shift from a land-dominant to water-dominant environment in the Isle de Jean Charles region. Straight cuts through the land forming maintained water channels for industry represent man's mark on the otherwise amphibious wet and dry zones.

At the far right, signs adjacent to the single two-lane road entry onto the Isle de Jean Charles were made and put in place by the remaining community. Their message: "We are not moving off this island..."

Buoyant Shadow

A cultural marker manifests as a floating mat of spherical marine buoys tethered to the ground below. The anchoring pattern marches along the submerged earthen levees marking the historic edge of water and land. Variations in buoy color and size mark the settlement pattern that once was. The marker, generated purely for cultural expression and longevity, over time takes on new meaning.

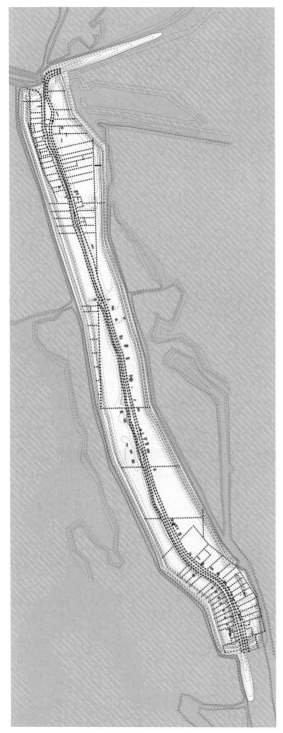
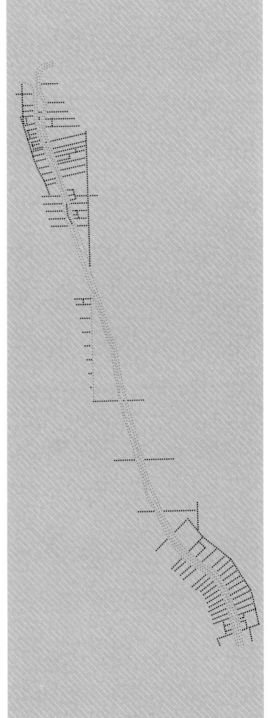

74

Oak Specter

Merging ecology and time, existing communities can plan for a prolonged cultural existence through ecological markings. While the community of Isle de Jean Charles maintains settlement on dry ground, native southern red oak trees are planted to mark individual parcels, property lines, and circulation patterns. As surrounding water levels rise, the oak trees mature. The ecological system once generated from fresh water and dry land's dominance slowly dies from salt and saltwater exposure. The trees' new growth dies, but the body of trunk and branches remains, marking the settlement that once was.

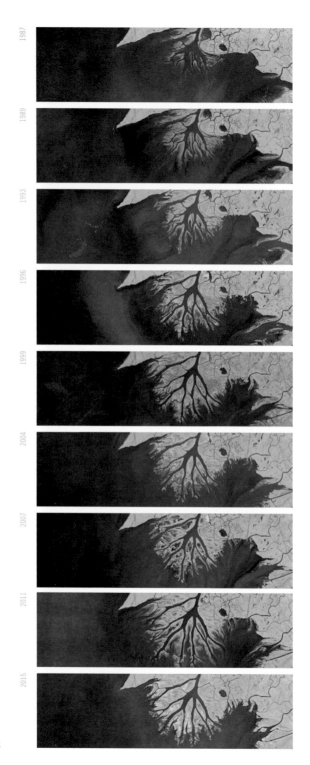

1987
1989
1993
1996
1999
2004
2007
2011
2015

Concurrent progradation and erosion over
time at the mouth of Wax Lake in Louisiana.

REMAPPING TERRITORY WITHOUT PLACE

Amphibious spaces must be cultivated in the present and planned for the future through practices of coexistence with aquatic environments rather than control of them. Planners, policy makers, insurers, architects, engineers, and builders must ask complex questions and innovate to engage littoral structures and settlements. The people and communities pressured by the rising sea will need to make a difficult decision: to leave behind their heritage and start anew or, alternatively, to envision an altered existence of inhabiting the rising water.

If history is understood not just as a sequence of actions but also as the accumulation of reactions across time, then design is both the production of space flush with potential and the mitigation of negative outcomes. Architecture must reframe current ecological, urban, political, and cultural protocols and recognize that the slow rendering of potential into consequence is a design(ed) process.

Pamphlet Architecture was initiated in 1977 as an independent vehicle to criticize, question, and exchange views. Each issue is assembled by an individual author, architect, or collective.

For information, Pamphlet proposals, or contributions, please write to: Pamphlet Architecture, c/o Princeton Architectural Press, 202 Warren Street, Hudson, NY 12534, or go to www.pamphletarchitecture.org.

Pamphlets published:

1.
Bridges
S. Holl, 1977*

2.
10 California Houses
M. Mack, 1978*

3.
Villa Prima Facie
L. Lerup, 1978*

4.
Stairwells
L. Dimitriu, 1979*

5.
Alphabetical City
S. Holl, 1980

6.
Einstein Tomb
L. Woods, 1980*

7.
Bridge of Houses
S. Holl, 1981*

8.
Planetary Architecture
Z. Hadid, 1981*

9.
Rural and Urban House Types
S. Holl, 1981*

10.
Metafisica della Architettura
A. Sartoris, 1984*

11.
Hybrid Buildings
J. Fenton, 1985

12.
Building: Machines
R. McCarter, 1987

13.
Edge of a City
S. Holl, 1991

14.
Mosquitoes
K. Kaplan, T. Krueger, 1993

15.
War and Architecture
L. Woods, 1993

16.
Architecture as a Translation of Music
E. Martin, 1994**

17.
Small Buildings
M. Caldwell, 1996

19.
Reading Drawing Building
M. Silver, 1996**

20.
Seven Partly Underground Rooms
M. A. Ray, 1997

21.
Situation Normal...
Lewis. Tsurumaki. Lewis, 1998

22.
Other Plans
Michael Sorkin Studio, 2001

23.
Move
J. S. Dickson, 2002

24.
Some Among Them Are Killers
D. Ross, 2003

25.
Gravity
J. Cathcart et al., 2003

26.
13 Projects for the Sheridan Expressway
J. Solomon, 2004

27.
Tooling
Aranda/Lasch, 2006

28.
Augmented Landscapes
Smout Allen, 2007

29.
Ambiguous Spaces
Naja & deOstos, 2008

30.
Coupling
InfraNet Lab / Lateral Office, 2010

31.
New Haiti Villages
S. Holl, 2011

32.
Resilience
Stasus, 2012

33.
Islands and Atolls
L. Callejas / LCLA Office, 2013

34.
Fathoming the Unfathomable
N. Chard & P. Kulper, 2013

35.
Going Live
P. Bélanger / OPSYS, 2015

36.
Buoyant Clarity
C. Meyer, S. Meyer, D. Hemmendinger, 2018

*out of print, available only in the collection Pamphlet Architecture 1–10.
**out of print, available only in the collection Pamphlet Architecture 11–20.

Selected Bibliography

Bejan, Adrian, and J. Peder Zane. *Design in Nature: How the Constructal Law Governs Evolution in Biology, Physics, Technology, and Social Organizations*. New York: Random House, 2012.

Cheramie, Kristi Dykema. "The Scale of Nature: Modeling the Mississippi River." *Places*. March 2011. http://placesjournal .org/article/the-scale-of-nature-modeling-the-mississippi-river.

Cobb, James C. *The Most Southern Place on Earth: The Mississippi Delta and the Roots of Regional Identity*. New York: Oxford University Press, 1992.

Corner, James. *Recovering Landscape: Essays in Contemporary Landscape Architecture*. New York: Princeton Architectural Press, 1999.

Glahn, Ben. "'Climate Refugees'?: Addressing the International Legal Gaps—Part II." International Bar Association. August 3, 2009. http://www.ibanet.org/Article/NewDetail .aspx?ArticleUid=3e9db1b0-659e-432b-8eb9-c9aeea53e4f6.

Jacobs, Jane. *The Death and Life of Great American Cities*. New York: Modern Library, 2011.

League of Nations. Records and Texts of the Conference for the Unification of Buoyage and Lighting of Coasts. Lisbon. October 6–23, 1930. Document no. C.163.M.58.1931.VIII.

Marshall, Amy K. "A History of Buoys and Tenders." Coast Guard Lighthouses. United States Coast Guard, January 12, 2016. http://www.uscg.mil/history/articles/BuoysTenders.pdf.

McPhee, John. *The Control of Nature*. Thorndike: G. K. Hall, 1999.

O'Brien, Greg. "Making the Mississippi River Over Again: The Development of River Control in Mississippi." *Mississippi History Now*. March 2002. http://mshistorynow.mdah.state .ms.us/articles/94/making-the-mississippi-river-over-again.

Parker, Laura. "Ocean Trash: 5.25 Trillion Pieces and Counting, but Big Questions Remain." *National Geographic*. January 11, 2015. http://news.nationalgeographic.com /news/2015/01/150109-oceans-plastic-sea-trash-science -marine-debris.

Reed, Chris, and Nina-Marie E. Lister. *Projective Ecologies*. New York: Actar, 2014.

Toole, John M., Michael S. McCartney, Nelson Hogg, and Robert A. Weller. "Outposts in the Ocean." *Oceanus* 42, no. 1 (2000). http://www.whoi.edu/oceanus/viewArticle.do?id=242.

Twain, Mark. *Life on the Mississippi*. Boston: James R. Osgood & Co., 1883.

Vitruvius, Pollio. *The Ten Books on Architecture*. Translated by Morris Hickey Morgan. New York: Dover, 1960.

Waldheim, Charles. *The Landscape Urbanism Reader*. New York: Princeton Architectural Press, 2006.

"Where Is All of the Earth's Water?" National Oceanic and Atmospheric Administration, National Ocean Service. Accessed June 3, 2016. http://oceanservice.noaa.gov.

Yoos, Jennifer, Vincent James, and Andrew Blauvelt. *Parallel Cities: The Multilevel Metropolis*. Minneapolis: Walker Art Center, 2016.

Image Credits

[p. 4] Image courtesy of NASA/JPL-Caltech.

[p. 7] (top) Image courtesy of Dan Lundberg, used under CC BY-SA 2.0. http://www.flickr.com/photos/9508280@ N07/25743479076/.

[p. 7] (bottom) Image by Jeffrey Shaw and Theo Botschuijver, Waterwalk Tube, Groningen, Netherlands, 1972.

[p. 8] (top) Image courtesy of the US Navy/JOC Fred J. Klinkenberger

[p. 8] (bottom series) Images courtesy of US Navy/John F. Williams.

[p. 11] (top) Image courtesy of Taco Witte, used under CC BY 2.0. http://www.flickr.com/photos/31817492@ N00/5441152878/.

[p. 11] (bottom) Image courtesy of the US Department of Energy.

[p. 13] Image courtesy of the Skyscraper Museum.

[p. 14] Image courtesy of Regional Plan Association.

[p. 16–17] Images courtesy of VJAA.

[p. 24–25] Images courtesy of the City of Morgan City.

[p. 38] Image courtesy of the government of the Maldives.

[p. 48] Photograph by Albert Brichaut.

[p. 64] Image courtesy of the SMU Central University Libraries.

[p. 71] (top) Image courtesy of Mohamed Affan, used under CC BY 2.0. http://www.flickr.com/photos/afu007/2391493378/.

Acknowledgments

We would like to thank the following institutions and organizations for their financial support in research and content development for this publication: Princeton Architectural Press and the University of Arkansas, Fay Jones School of Architecture + Design.

The work found in this publication would not have been possible without the contributions of a great many people. We thank Erin Cox, Sarah Gunawan, Davis Owen, Fani-Christina Papadopoulou, and Sonny Xu for their assistance with the design and graphic development of this work.

Jennifer Yoos, Vincent James, and Kiel Moe helped orient and complete the trajectory of this publication. Their contributions represent only a fraction of their support. We sincerely thank them.

We appreciate our colleagues for their generosity, creative input, and late night conversations during the production of this book: Justin Merkovich, Erin Hester, Alex Shelly, Martin Finio, Taryn Christoff, Caleb Linville, Jenna Dezinski, Mike Kuntz, Janelle Kuntz, Mike Johnson, Jessica Johnson, and Xiangyun (Faye) Wang.

We also thank our families for their tireless support and encouragement as we pursue the curiosities of architecture.

A special thank you to Fani-Christina Papadopoulou for her thoughtfulness, command, rigor, and buoyant spirit.

Buoyant Clarity is dedicated to Evan and Wyatt Meyer for their enduring patience and comic relief. Thank you boys; you are inspiring.